PRAISE FOR
PAUL FERRINI'S BOOKS

"The most important book I have read. I study it like a bible!"
Elisabeth Kubler-Ross, M.D.

"These words embody tolerance, universality, love and compassion—hallmarks of all Great Teachings. They turn our attention inward to our own divine nature, instead of diverting it outward. Paul Ferrini is a modern-day Kahlil Gibran—poet, mystic, visionary, teller of truth." Larry Dossey, M.D.

"Paul Ferrini leads us skillfully and courageously beyond shame, blame and attachment to our wounds into the depths of self-forgiveness. His work is a must-read for all people who are ready to take responsibility for their own healing."
John Bradshaw

"A breath of fresh air in an often musty and cluttered domain. With sweetness, clarity, and simplicity we are directed to the truth within. I read this book whenever my heart directs, which is often." Pat Rodegast

"Paul Ferrini's writing is authentic, delightful and wise. It reconnects the reader to the Spirit Within, to that place where even our deepest wounds can be healed."
Joan Borysenko, Ph.D.

"I feel that this work comes from a continuous friendship with the deepest part of the Self. I trust its wisdom."
Coleman Barks, poet and translator.

"Paul Ferrini's wonderful books show a way to walk lightly with joy on planet earth." Gerald Jampolsky, M.D.

"Paul Ferrini leads us on a gentle journey to our true source of joy and happiness—inside ourselves." Ken Keyes, Jr.

Cover Design by Elizabeth Lewis & Paul Ferrini
Cover Photograph by Maggie Le Duc, President of Healing
Images, Inc., A Torrance California Corporation.
Other photography by Eleanor LeBlanc
Typesetting by Kay Yamaguchi

ISBN 1-879159-03-1

Second Printing, March 1994

~~

Manufactured in the United States of America

THE BRIDGE TO REALITY

PAUL FERRINI

"Conflict must be resolved. It cannot be evaded, set aside, denied, disguised, seen somewhere else, called by another name, or hidden by deceit of any kind, if it would be escaped. It must be seen as it is, where it is thought to be, in the reality which has been given it, and with the purpose that the mind accorded it. For only then are its defenses lifted, and the truth can shine upon it as it disappears."

A Course in Miracles Workbook Lesson 333

Table of Contents

~

INTRODUCTION

This Book concerns itself with the application in daily life of the principles elucidated in *A Course in Miracles,* a work of contemporary scripture received by Helen Schucman in the period 1965-1972. The spiritual principles presented by the *Course* are not essentially different than the ones taught by Jesus some two thousand years ago. This is not surprising, since Jesus claims to be the author of the *Course,* and anyone taking the time to read this extraordinary document will find striking similarities to the teaching of Jesus as told in the gospels.

The *Course,* however, is not just theory, but also practice. It presents us with a road map for exploring our judgments, our fears, and our guilt. It asks us to look at and take responsibility for every thought we have, especially when we are feeling pain and separation. If we look deeply enough, we will see that all our negative emotional states stem from the belief that we are not worthy of love. Since this belief is buried in our emotional body, it tends to surface in our awareness only when we feel criticized, attacked, rejected, or betrayed. *The Course* tells us that defending ourselves against our brother's attack or blaming him for our upset will never bring us peace. If we want peace, we must be willing to look for the source of our upset inside ourselves.

Many students of *the Course* and similar paths underestimate the depth of emotional work required to undo the habitual patterns of attack and defense which create suffering in their lives. Attempting to skip over their emotional healing, they often develop a strong persona of spirituality, while inside they still carry deep shame and unforgiveness of themselves. Sooner or later these deepset feelings of unworthiness must be brought to light and released.

The passageway to emotional healing lies in our willingness to look at our woundedness when it comes up. We do this, not to wallow in our pain, but so we can see the ways in which we push love away in our attempt to protect ourselves from hurt and loss. Until we see our ego's patterns of defense, we cannot dismantle the thick walls we have built around our hearts.

No matter what path you are on, there is always a profound difference between theory and practice. Many people spend their lives arguing about whose theory is the best, but never begin to practice their spiritual beliefs. This is no less true for students of *A Course in Miracles* than it is for students of any other teaching or tradition. In the final analysis it is not till the heart opens that real progress on our spiritual path begins.

There is nothing esoteric or mystical about this. The more we accept and embrace our lives and the people in them as they are, the more we begin to feel Love's presence. And the more we feel this presence, the more our hearts open.

The approach to spirituality presented in this book is heart centered and experiential. It talks not just about concepts, but about how these concepts can be integrated into daily life. Often, I share stories from my own life to help you make this connection.

I offer this book to you with the request that you be

gentle on yourself as you read it. Your acceptance of yourself moment to moment is the greatest gift that you can give to yourself on your spiritual journey. The process of coming to embrace yourself wholly and completely requires great sensitivity, patience, and courage. We all need to honor this process until it bears fruit. Our vineyard flowers when we tend to it faithfully. Of this, we can be sure.

The "bridge" in the title of this book represents the transition we are making from pretense to authenticity, from illusion to Reality. As we let go of the persona we constructed in fear, we begin to acknowledge and communicate the truth about ourselves. And the truth is that who we are is not subject to what other people think about us, or how they treat us. None of us is a victim of another person, even though we may be extremely good at playing this role. As soon as we decide we are unwilling to be victimized, the game is over. It only takes one person to break the chain of abuse.

As we learn to honor who we are, it is not difficult to honor others. And only then do we begin to move across the Bridge to Reality, dropping our disguises, defenses, and grievances. Gradually, we abandon the old way of thinking and feeling based on manipulation and control and grope toward a new way of being based on trust and faith.

The bridge seems to exist in the world, but that too is appearance. Everyone we meet just reflects back to us what we believe about ourselves. The Bridge to Reality is not external, but within our hearts and minds. As we cross that bridge we move beyond personal agendas and attachments to a heart-felt compassion for anyone in the grip of fear, including ourselves.

When we stop pretending to be holier than Thou, we discover who the wounded one is. That is the beginning of our healing journey. Then we start to tell the truth. We start to share our real stories. We meet in the middle of our pain and take each other's hand. We learn to forgive, and we understand that, despite our mistakes, we are worthy of love. You are my witness and I am yours. Blessed be the moment in when we look into each other's eyes and see the truth reflected. For that is a holy act. That is an act of grace.

Paul Ferrini
Santa Fe, New Mexico

All God Asks is That We Open Our Hearts

MOVING THROUGH FEAR TO LOVE

Every moment of fear blocks our awareness of love's presence.

Yet if we do not deny fear (by repressing it or projecting it), it melts away. Fear is the beginning of separation. If we deny our fear we separate further, creating an enemy outside and an unnecessary schism between heart and mind within. But if we dwell in that moment without resistance, we will see that our fear is entirely subjective. It has no reality apart from us.

Fear comes from us and we create our beliefs out of it. Fear stands behind all our beliefs in separation, and 99% of our beliefs are beliefs in separation. Most of those beliefs fall into the category "I am not Okay" or "You are not Okay." The existence of either confirms the other and demonstrates our overall conviction that separation is real.

Fear is the ephemeral monster that guards the gate to hell itself. When we run from it, it chases us. Only when we stand our ground do we realize that it is without substance. Only when we stand our ground do we invite the darkness in and bring it to the light.

Fear creates my world, but I do not know it. This is another way of saying I create my world, but I do not know it. I do not know it because I do not stay with my fear long enough to know that it comes from me.

Fear comes from me, but I do not recognize it. I think it comes from you (I project it) or I pretend it isn't

15

there (I deny it).

The problem with projecting fear is that it brings conflict into my relationships. When fear is in my relationships, I forget that it started in myself.

The problem with denying fear is that I deny my feelings. I intellectualize. I create a pretense which I'm always struggling to validate. I create a schism within myself. I teach myself that what I feel isn't real.

It is ironic. I never come to know fear, because I am afraid of it. I'm always getting rid of it before I experience it.

I am afraid of fear. I am afraid of what I do not know. That is it, quite simply. Fear is the door to the unknown. It is the gateway of the mystery. Being with my fear is the first step across the Bridge to Reality.

In so doing, I leave behind what I think I know. I expect my fear to intensify, but it does not. Ironically, the more I move toward the unknown, the more my fear begins to diminish.

I am terrified of the unknown, yet the more I walk toward it the less I fear. This is the inversion of all my old beliefs.

Staying with my fear does not deepen it. Staying with my fear dissolves it.

Leaving what I know does not make me more afraid. It makes me less afraid. Now, I am moving across The Bridge.

I cross The Bridge in the Holy Instant. I stay with my feelings. I do not deny how I feel. I do not project what I feel. I remain here, centered in the moment, and I ascend.

I leave the world my fear has created — the world

"Love does not wait upon us to perform its miracles, nor does it try to coerce us out of our stubborn resistance. It simply offers us again and again the opportunity to trust in what we are."

that I know— and enter the world that I did not create — the world of my innocence. In that world I know nothing. All I can do is say with God "It is Good. I am Okay." That is all. More than that is not necessary.

More than that is a movement into judgment. More than that means leaving the garden, like Adam and Eve did, feeling embarrassment and shame.

More than that is not necessary.

In my innocence, fear is impossible. What was once fear is now sufficiency. I am whole. I am complete. I am as you are. There can be no difference between us.

When fear dissolves, so does all sense of separation.

Moses felt fear, but he had the courage to walk with it. As he walked, the people of Israel followed. As they walked, the waters of the Red Sea stood aside to let them pass. Walking through our fear is the first gesture of healing.

Every moment exists in "the garden" or in "the fall from grace."

In every moment, we walk through our fear to reality, or we run from it into illusion. Every moment is a choice for separation or union, for fear or love.

Every moment offers us a Bridge to Reality. Will we cross over or remain with our pain? That is our continual choice.

In time, we will all cross this bridge. In truth, we have already crossed it. For Reality is our nature.

In time, we will uncover the blocks to love's presence one by one. We think those blocks are outside of us, but that is hardly the case. The Bridge to Reality is not outside, but within.

Welcome to the threshold of the heart, where all return

to the One. Welcome home, brother and sister. Here you are forgiven. Here you are blessed. Om Shanti. Peace be to All. Peace is All. Only Peace. Peace. Peace.

"PEACE IS THE BRIDGE"

If you take the time to listen, you will know that peace can be felt within. Peace is the flower of silence. It is deep acceptance of yourself and everyone. It is all inclusive.

Reject one person, remain angry toward one person and you cannot feel your peace. Feel guilty, sad, neglected and you cannot feel your peace.

You enter your peace when you leave all these thoughts and feelings of separation behind. Peace is there when judgment drops away. It deepens when concepts melt away. It opens its heart to you when words and thoughts cease.

In peace is acceptance total. In peace is bliss total. Listen deeply and you will feel this. It is your nature. It is who you are. Everything else is an artifice, an add on, an illusion. Only your peace is real.

In daily life, many situations come up which seem to take your peace away. Ah, but remember, only peace is real, so how can it be taken away? It cannot be. It can only be covered up.

Every time we have an expectation, we cover it up. Every time we assume that we know something, we cover it up. Every time we judge ourselves or someone else,

19

we cover it up. When we resist, project, withdraw, attack or defend, we cover up our peace. In telling us to "choose for our peace," *The Course* reminds us that our Peace is always accessible to us.

Choosing our peace means choosing against our pain. We would all like our pain to go away by itself, but that is just wishful thinking. If we want our pain to go away, we need to choose peace. Choosing peace dissolves our pain. In choosing one, we negate the other.

Everything happens by our permission. We choose what makes us happy. And we choose what makes us miserable. *The Course* says: "There are no neutral thoughts." Every thought is a choice for peace or a choice for pain.

The choice for peace is the only choice we need to make. Once we have chosen peace, we can extend it, including others in its gentle embrace.

By sharing our peace, we reconfirm it. That is what our journey here is all about: discovering peace within and sharing it without. There is nothing more than this.

Anything other than this just covers up our peace and then we have to dis-cover it again. That's okay. Every mistake we make is a great learning device, allowing us to come back on track with greater intensity.

When I judge myself for covering up my peace, I bury it more deeply. When I forgive myself for covering it up, I discover it again.

In this moment, I discover my peace or make it inaccessible. All of the pain of the past is dissolved when I choose peace here and now.

FINDING FAULT

The Course is explicit that my experience of peace depends on my ability to see my brother's sinlessness. This makes perfect sense to us, but why is it so difficult to practice?

Why do I have such a strong tendency to find fault with my sister? Why is it so easy for me to believe that she can attack me and hurt me? When I love my sister, why do I feel so vulnerable? When I praise and honor her, why do I feel that I diminish myself?

Am I really as small and powerless as I feel in relationship to my brother? Of course not! But my need to find fault with him shows me that I feel powerless. I feel unworthy. I feel unappreciated. I feel un-loved.

That is my psychological state. My judgment and attack of my sister is simply a compensation for my feeling of lack of wholeness, my fear that I can be further diminished, separated, judged. I need to understand this.

Inside me is a little child who is afraid. That child is in you too. If you don't see her, then you are in denial. Sorry, but that hurt, angry, confused, lonely child is more real than all of your "adult" images of self. That child has an emotional integrity that simply must be honored. Until it is, the adult part of you will be an empty shell, undernourished emotionally, an artifice of mind without "gut" or heart energy.

It is the hurt child that attacks. See your inner child, feel him, and you will understand how all that need to attack is just a call for love and attention.

When your sister finds fault with you it is her hurt child calling for love and acceptance. See it that way and it will be easier for you to respond gently, lovingly.

If you have children, see if you can meet their attack with love. Perhaps you do not know it, but they learn attack from you. Teach love by giving it to your children. That is the greatest gift you can give to them.

Think for a moment what it would have been like had your parents given that gift to you. That is an awesome thought, is it not? Of course, they tried. They did the best that they could. But often their own wounded child got in the way. Often, they looked to you to meet their needs and your needs were overlooked.

This is not about judgment. It is about understanding. We all need to understand the love starved child within, the one who feels inadequate, the one who feels angry and neglected. Understanding this part of us helps us own it. When we own it, we don't have to blame our parents anymore. And we don't have to blame ourselves either.

You see this child is restless. He wants our attention. He wants his emotional needs met. It is time. Now, perhaps he realizes that he has the ability to meet those needs directly.

Instead of looking for love from others, our child learns to offer it to himself. It is hard, but gradually the child begins to say "I'm really Okay. I deserve love, and I want to be loving to myself."

The adult cannot begin to fulfill her creative purpose until the inner child has been healed. The work of self-acceptance begins with the recognition and nurturing of the child within.

Practicing the perception of our brother's sinlessness is intricately linked to our discovery of our own. Until we truly accept ourselves emotionally, how can we accept others?

We want to make this an outer journey, but it cannot be. We want to forgive our brothers and sisters, but if we are honest we know that our forgiveness of them is superficial. That is because we haven't forgiven ourselves. It just isn't possible to offer our brother or sister what we have not been able to offer to ourselves.

The Course is clear about this. The unhealed healer cannot heal. If we want to be vehicles for healing, we must begin by forgiving ourselves.

I can pretend that I live in the light all the time, but if I keep getting angry, judging and attacking, then I can be sure that I have not come to grips with my dark side. I cannot bring this dark side into the light until I accept it.

Yes, you see, I am just a child. I am learning. I still have all these irrational needs and emotional reactions. I hurt. I lash out. I defend myself. I am just like you, brother.

I don't have to be holier than you. I don't have to make you holier than me. We are equals. We are on the journey together. We are learning together. I need your help. You need mine. It is Okay. We'll get there. We'll help each other get there.

That is how we make a place for the child. That is how we embrace our darkness and bring it to the light. That is how we witness for each other.

THE HEROIC JOURNEY

The journey of spirit takes us into our feelings, not away from them. We do not uncover our peace by pretending our pain isn't there. Being with our pain enables us to move through it. Being with our grief helps us express it. Being with our anger helps us own it so that we can let it go.

When we claim our feelings, we become energized and centered. When we deny them or rationalize them, we divide ourselves in half. What is the unconscious after all but an umbrella word for all the aspects of self we have denied?

Feelings are our friends, not our enemies. They tell us where we are here and now. They help us reclaim the present. Being with our feelings is just being present, being here in the fullness of our being.

Accepting our feelings creates a movement toward alignment. The feeling may be a message to us that misalignment exists, but the acceptance of the feeling allows the centering process to begin.

When we acknowledge our feelings, they help us open the door to healing.

The inability to honor and accept our feelings takes us out of the present into a fantasy world. The world of denial is one dimensional and stiff. It consists of automatic, stereotyped responses to people and situations. That is because it has been robbed of feeling.

A mind that relies primarily on the analytical, left brain qualities of the psyche is a mechanical mind. A world created by a mind cut off from its feeling nature is a barren world.

It is a world in which man is separated from himself. William Blake described this separation in the story of Urizen, his prophetic vision of western man as a head without a body. Later, T.S. Elliot painted a similar portrait of modern man in "The Hollow Men" and "The Wasteland."

Feeling is the binding agent of the psyche. It brings integration. Our sense of Self is a feeling tone, more than a set of ideas. It is unpredictable and rich. It has a full spectrum of possibilities before it and it is spontaneous in exercising them.

Acceptance of our feelings brings us into the heart. This is the place where love begins. In being with our feelings, we witness our own capacity for violence and betrayal. We see own our destructive tendencies. By owning these feelings, we no longer need to project them. We go beyond the "Us Good Guys Vs. Those Bad Guys" syndrome. We begin to acknowledge our sisterhood with all beings.

This is very different from an intellectual commitment to the concept of equality. It comes from a deep inner honesty, an emotional integrity, not from a beautiful concept which we have trouble integrating in our own lives.

By being with our own feelings, we find it easier to accept the feelings of others without being threatened by them. You see, this is where love starts, when we can be with someone, when we can be there fully, without judging. That is true support for our sister. That is the soil in which love flowers.

The heroic journey starts at home with what you are feeling right now. It demands inner honesty. Its asks for your willingness to share what you feel. It invites your brother into your heart. Compassion is its basis. Gentleness is its basis. As you extend in this way, gentleness and compassion return to you.

TRUST AND EMPOWERMENT

Our ability to trust others depends on our willingness to trust ourselves. Yet self trust is not as easy as it sounds.

In most cases, we grow up looking for guidance outside ourselves. We project our power onto other people, losing touch with our intuitive understanding of life as it happens. Or we project our power onto abstract concepts and try to live our life through their mold. The projection of our power onto people or ideas works against the development of self trust. And self trust is the beginning of self empowerment.

If I want to trust myself I must see you clearly. I cannot see you clearly if I project my power onto you or allow you to project your power onto me. Only when we meet as equals is trust possible.

My trust in myself and my trust in you is not mutually exclusive. When I trust you, I automatically trust myself. When I trust you I cannot be disappointed in anything that you do, because I know that you did the best you could.

It is a moot idea to think that I can or should withdraw my trust because "you disappointed me." The very experience of "disappointment" is a withdrawal of trust. When I am disappointed in you, I no longer trust you. And I no longer trust myself. I think I was wrong to trust you.

Now I have made both of us wrong. Not trusting is a "no win" situation.

Trusting is a "no lose" situation. When I trust you, I recognize your good intentions regardless of the outcome of a situation. I continue to trust even when I see that my expectations have not been met. I know that there is no relationship between my trust in you and your inability to meet my expectations.

Trusting is a continual choice. We don't trust each other once and then find that trust is there in all our interactions. All our interactions offer us the opportunity to extend our trust or to step out of trust into separation.

Trust flowers in the soil of equality. Trust happens naturally when we meet as equals. When we don't, suspicion and mistrust dominate.

Suspicion and mistrust for another person reflect our inability to trust ourselves. I can't trust you if I don't trust myself.

When I trust myself, I extend that trust to you automatically. I know you are equal to me. I honor you as an equal even if you try to tell me that you are not.

Artificial power, the kind of "power" that attacks, manipulates and humiliates comes from the perception of inequality. Power struggles take place only between non-equals. Non equals always seek to be equals, although they may not realize it consciously. That is what the "struggle" is all about. It will continue until both parties recognize their equality.

Inequality seeks equality. Disharmony seeks harmony. Illusions seek Reality. The false seeks the true. How else could it be?

Artificial power yields to the power of the Self. The power of the Self cannot be compromised. It cannot be in conflict with the power of another Self. The power of each is the same power. The power of the Self is total in each of us precisely because it is totally shared. It belongs to all of us equally. In this way, God's Will abides within us.

The personal moves toward the impersonal. You cannot avoid it. The ability to love one person moves toward the ability to love all. Each act of love in your life is symbolic of universal love.

～

TAKING RESPONSIBILITY

Reality is Self reflecting. Everything in your life reflects who you are. All the people in your life reflect attitudes and beliefs you have about yourself. Seen as it is, Reality reveals you as a creator of your world.

When we see in this way, we see from the perspective of Truth. Our sight is no longer limited to what the body's eyes see, nor do we see other beings as bodies. We have moved beyond that.

We see life not as we think it should be, nor as we want it to be, but as it is. We no longer add the illusory burden of our perception to what we see, and so we look on what is. We also know that everything we see in truth is meant to bless. And when we do not find blessings before us, we understand that once again the curtain of illusion has descended before our eyes.

When we see from truth we take total responsibility for every situation in our lives. There are no exceptions. Every situation, every relationship, every event reflects the consciousness that created it.

Three dimensional experience is transitional. It moves forwards toward the fourth dimension (transcending the limits of time/space), or backwards toward duality. In each moment, we decide which direction we will take. Projection is a movement back toward duality. Responsibility is a movement forward toward realization.

We all need to understand that we are here in three-dimensional reality because we need to learn to take responsibility for our lives. At first, we deny responsibility and try to make others responsible for what happens in our lives. This just deepens our pain and our feelings of powerlessness. Then, we begin to take responsibility for ourselves in little ways. This empowers us. It pushes us beyond old limitations. It expands our consciousness about who we are. It brings us a step closer to truth.

Taking responsibility always empowers us. Projecting responsibility always weakens us. Taking responsibility helps us give birth to the Self so that we can share It with others. Projecting responsibility causes us to look for acceptance from others, a search which is as futile when it works as it is when it doesn't.

No amount of external acceptance can replace our ability to accept ourselves in the depth of our being. Such acceptance leads to responsibility, not away from it. Whether we are alone or with a partner, we will face the need for self-affirmation again and again until we fulfill it. This is a need that we all have and must meet sooner or later.

Becoming responsible for our lives means coming to grips with our power to create. It does not matter whether we choose to become responsible for our lives while living alone or while living with another person. Either way, we make the choice that sets us free.

Whoever takes responsibility for what she creates in her life releases all other beings from judgment or blame. She is loved, for she owns what she creates, and forgives herself when what she creates does not affirm who she is. Her self-forgiveness encourages our own. Thus, wherever she walks, she blesses and is blessed.

Three dimensional reality is relational. It is a mutual conspiracy between us for awakening from limitation. You help me see the Self I cannot see. You help me face my blind spots so I can go beyond them. And you help me see the Goodness in me I cannot see through the veil of self-judgment. Without your presence, I could not awaken.

Moving from three dimensional reality to four dimensional reality is the work of inner integration. It involves a synthesis of opposites within the Self. Realization flows forth from this synthesis. Realization is the birth of the whole Self, neither male nor female, but androgynous. Light does not oppose the darkness, but illumines it.

It is not the work of projection, but the end of projection. Responsibility can be taken only when the need for projection has been outgrown. Then there is only Self. And everything around it reflects it.

ALL ATTACK IS SELF ATTACK

Three dimensional reality is all about the movement toward self-abuse or self-recognition. Abusing myself begins under the guise of abusing you. I can never attack myself directly. If I did that, I would promptly wake up.

Instead, I attack you. You become the object for the assault of my self-hatred.

If I listen to my feelings, I realize that I am dreadfully unhappy. I admit my unhappiness, but I won't take responsibility for it: " Yes, it is true that I am unhappy, but it is your fault."

Projection keeps the cycle of attack alive. Only when I take responsibility for my own present happiness or lack of it, can I break through the thin facade of self deceit and see that my attack against you is really an attack against myself. Then, and only then, do I begin to awaken.

To heal I must find out the simple but difficult fact that I am the cause of my unhappiness. Until I know that, all of my relationships will be twisted by conflict and projection.

Relationships mirror what we bring to them. If we bring inner conflict, we see that conflict materialized in our interactions. If we bring self-acceptance and responsibility, we experience real understanding and communication.

Three dimensional reality is neither bad nor good. It is a stage in our learning process that simply offers us the opportunity to see ourselves as we really are.

Relationships can be hurtful or helpful, depending on what we bring to them, depending on our courage to grow and open up emotionally. They "up the ante" on our growth and development.

Co-dependent relationships exacerbate the pain that results from our ego-based reality. They give us a taste of love, but it always comes with strings attached. Those strings strangle the spirit of both partners. They deepen the pain and make growth impossible.

Yet all our unholy relationships are moving toward holiness. Even our most difficult relationships bring us to the place where our choice is clear: we either find a new way of being together or we lose faith in our ability to love and be loved.

Finding our faith in love means being willing to trust it. For most of us, this is a new experience. We don't yet know what love means. We know how to imprison one another, but we don't know how to set each other free.

It is awkward at first, but we can and do learn. Love teaches us about love. Indeed, nothing else can teach us.

Love takes us from the conditional to the unconditional, from the premeditated to the spontaneous, from the partial to the total. You can't love anyone just a little bit or when it is convenient.

Love does not wait upon us to perform its miracles, nor does it try to coerce us out of our stubborn resistance. It simply offers us again and again the opportunity to trust in what we are.

EMBRACING THE SHADOW

The process of learning to trust ourselves and each other is item number one on the agenda for all of us. It takes us into scary places, where we come face to face with our power issues. Confronting our perceptions of inequality means looking at our capacity for violence. We do this not to reinforce it, but to recognize it so we can stop projecting it.

A *Course in Miracles* tells us quite emphatically that our darkness, our capacity for violence is not real. It is true that our fears, our alienation, our pain, our separation do not belong to the eternal, ultimate reality. They are not part of God and so they are ultimately unreal.

But they are part of our mental/emotional reality. They characterize our existence in this limited, conditional world. While we have these feelings, it does not help us to deny them. Pretending they do not exist will not get rid of them. The way to peace is not through denial. It is through acceptance.

Where is the bridge between the conditional world and the unconditional world? It is in my acceptance of my feelings, here and now. That is the entrance into the Holy Instant.

When I recognize truly and openly my tendency to attack and be attacked, I can begin to move across the bridge. Accepting the truth about where I am gives me a place to work from. Pretending to be where I am not keeps me chained to the cycle of violence.

That is why in the Twelve Step programs you start with the truth about yourself. You start by admitting and accepting where you are. Only then are you ready to move toward where you want to be.

All spiritual work starts with self honesty and self-acceptance.

Don't let anyone tell you that spiritual work begins with the denial of feelings. It just isn't true. Spiritual work begins not in pretense, but in deep, personal acceptance. That is the beginning of the conscious journey.

Stepping onto the bridge means bringing the darkness to the light, bringing the unconscious into consciousness. It means owning the journey.

~~

THE CONSCIOUS JOURNEY

Yes, my friend. I know now that all of my judgments and opinions of you are just ideas I have about myself. So let me not talk about you. I am the one who attacks. I am the one who defends.

I am the victim. I am the executioner. I am the angel of rescue.

I am the murderer, manipulator, helper and savior. There is nothing that can be that I have not been.

I have seen it all. I have done it all.

And, having seen and done it all, I have given up shame. I have given up blame.

No, I do not project my guilt onto you, friend. For I

34

know that there is nothing that has crossed your mind which I too have not contemplated.

I accept my darkness. I accept my light. This does not bring conflict.

My darkness shows where light is needed. My light yearns for the muscle of form.

Do not tell me there is no joy in this tapestry of light and shadow. Do not tell me that this mottled world has no beauty, for its beauty is mine, and so is its sadness.

Do not tell me that spirit and flesh are opposed. For the body is not evil and spirit is beyond the "good" with a small g.

When I accept the duality, I move into unity. All is "Good." All is "God" with a capital G.

Spirit/body terminology is a teaching device. Love moves us beyond this duality.

Love tells us that we are responsible for the journey. That means that the journey is dark only if we remain in darkness.

There is light and there is darkness in the dual world, the conditional world. Light and dark alternate. In each psyche, light comes and goes.

If I grab onto the light and deny the darkness, I have a false spirituality, an intellectual spirituality that cannot handle the emotional currents of my life. If I grab onto the darkness and deny the light, I paint myself into a narrow corner where I feel increasingly cut off from others. I lose hope. I feel suicidal. I have nothing to live for.

Nobody lives for the darkness. We live for the light, but we cannot have the light when we deny the darkness.

When we accept darkness and light together, a funny thing happens: we move into an awareness of light which is non-physical. It includes both the darkness and the light, but these no longer oscillate back and forth. The pendulum has stopped at the balance point. This is the light of truth, of compassion, the eternal light.

Accept the opposites and you merge into the One. Deny them and you perpetuate the conflict. This is the bridge.

SELF-ACCEPTANCE

The greatest block to my awareness of love's presence in my life is the idea that there is some aspect of myself which is unacceptable. This unacceptable aspect can be:

my sexuality,
my anger,
my fear,
my distrust,
my creativity,
my sensitivity,
my eating,
my drinking,
my competitiveness,
and so on.

The list is endless. It is slightly different for each person. Each list has both positive and negative aspects.

It may seem surprising, but all of us do not accept certain positive aspects of ourselves. Rather than develop and express these positive aspects, we project them onto someone else. For example, I marry a charismatic "artist" so that I don't have to develop and express my own creativity.

We also project negative aspects of ourselves. I always have problems with controlling, overbearing people (because I am that way myself). My anger at them is really anger at myself.

Not accepting any aspect of myself is a block to my awareness of love's presence in my life. I cannot love myself so long as there is any aspect of myself I do not accept.

"Accept all of yourself" is the first requirement for the spiritual journey. This means you embrace everything you like as well as everything you dislike about yourself.

Accepting all of yourself does not mean that you justify or condone your negative qualities. You simply recognize that they are there and accept this as a starting point. You own yourself. You divulge your secrets.

Next, you realize that everything that you like and everything you dislike is just an idea you have about yourself. Actually, you are not any of these ideas you have about yourself. All of these ideas comprise your self image. You can always change your self image. You can never change your self.

Once you have owned your darkness, your shadow self, you can begin to bring it to the light. By looking at the aspects of yourself you have previously disowned, you begin to make friends with them.

At first it is difficult. But behind every so called "negative" quality is a positive one that needs to be accepted and integrated into your being. Your previous judgment about this quality was based on fear. Now, as you begin to encounter it, you realize its essence was always positive.

All aspects of yourself are holy. As you work through your "images" of self, you begin to experience the Self that is beyond images, eternal and without form. This is a life long process.

The understanding that "I am acceptable exactly as I am" is the most profound understanding I can have. It opens the door to the heart.

As I find myself increasingly acceptable, I find it easier to accept you. In so doing, I experience my essential equality with you. Our relationship changes from one of conflict and distrust to one of cooperation and support. We offer each other the continual opportunity to love.

A holy relationship is simply one of complete equality. There can be no racism, sexism, prejudice or conceit of any kind in a holy relationship. In a holy relationship, I accept you totally as you are here and now.

"Accept others as they are" is the next requirement of the spiritual life. Judge them not. Replace all judgments of others with the practice of conscious acceptance.

The acceptance of self removes internal conflict. The acceptance of others removes external conflict. Each process enhances the other. This is very simple to understand. It is very hard to do.

That is why it is essential that we be gentle with ourselves and each other. We must not set impossible goals. We don't have to forgive all of the past all at once. We release the past in the present. That is all that we can do.

FORGIVENESS: THE TURNING POINT

Sometimes we try to accept ourselves and it doesn't work. Sometimes we try to accept others and it doesn't work. We can beat ourselves, run ourselves down and deepen our shame, or we can recognize our mistake and move on.

"I wanted to accept you but instead I got angry. Instead, I projected my stuff onto you."

"I wanted to accept myself, but instead of listening to the voice that blesses, I listened to the voice that condemns."

The voice of condemnation has two sides: the inferiority side and the superiority side. The former says: "I'm not as good as others. I'll never amount to anything." The superiority side says: "I'm better than so and so. I don't understand why he gets all the attention."

Both voices are asking for love. Yet both ask for love from an illusory stance of inequality. Neither voice addresses a sister. Both voices address a projection of our own making.

This happens all the time. And every time it happens it shows us our lack of genuine love for ourselves and others. We try to ask for love but we end up demanding it, or manipulating to get it. We make mistakes. Then we make more mistakes. And then we make more mistakes. We all know the process. We live it day to day.

This is where forgiveness comes in. Forgiveness is the Bridge to Reality.

Reality is our complete acceptance of ourselves and our brother. That is the goal. That is our true capacity. It is important to understand the goal, but we must not take the goal and use it to beat ourselves because we fall short of reaching it.

Do you think the ego will hesitate to use concepts of "God" or "love" or "acceptance" to beat you? Let's be honest. It happens all the time.

So, having recognized the goal, we must come to understand, value and practice the process. *A Course in Miracles* offers us a "process" in remembering who we are. It is a process of unlearning all the false concepts we have of ourselves and each other.

It is a process that can be undertaken only with great gentleness, for the ends and the means are the same. The goal of acceptance and the practice of acceptance are the same.

Whenever we find that we have separated the ends from the means, the goal from the process, we know that we have lost touch with the heart of Jesus' teaching. The heart of His teaching is forgiveness.

There is no problem, no situation, which cannot be addressed successfully through forgiveness. Every act of forgiveness removes a "block to the awareness of love's presence."

Love is present at all times. I am just not aware of it. I focus on other things. In separation, I move away from love. The further away I move, the more I judge, blame, attack, defend, and so on. I promote my own misery.

Forgiveness stops this downward spiral of self hatred.

It does not matter at what stage you find forgiveness. It may be in the beginning stages of self-blame. It may be at the moment in which you contemplate suicide. Forgiveness always works. It brings you the release from the downward spiral.

The more profound your pain, the more profound your forgiveness will be. The more subtle your suffering, the more subtle your forgiveness will be. You always get what you need.

What is forgiveness? It is your first act of responsibility! It is literally that. And so it is the turning point.

You see, no one else can forgive you. The forgiveness of others is necessary for them, not for you. Forgiving you is part of their healing process. No, others cannot forgive you. God cannot forgive you.

Remember that. God cannot forgive you. God did not create you sinful. S/He sees nothing to forgive. To ask God for forgiveness is to turn away from God.

No one can forgive you except you. That is why it is your first act of courage, your first act of love. Everything positive in your life stems from this simple but often profoundly difficult act.

Each act of forgiveness is a miracle. Without forgiveness, there can be no miracles.

When I forgive myself I stand up inside my life. I own my life. I own my feelings. I understand that all my mistakes are part of a learning process.

Mistakes are not bad. Nothing in my life is bad if I can learn from it. Even the most terrible things can be tools for forgiveness.

Pain is a gift if it brings me to self-acceptance. Suffering is a gift if it brings me to love. Anything in our lives can

"Each act of forgiveness is a miracle. Without forgiveness, there can be no miracles."

be used for healing. We must remember that.

It is far too easy to get hung up on the form of the gift. When we expect a gift to come only in a certain size or shape or modality, we miss its presence in our lives.

When we honor everything in our lives, we accept all of the gifts that come to us: even the ones we do not yet understand, even the ones that have yet to be revealed to us.

From the perspective of ultimate Reality suffering is not real. But if we feel suffering in our lives, we must learn to move through it.

Suffering is a process. Pain is a process. Mistakes are a process. Forgiveness is a process. Everything that does not belong to ultimate Reality is a process.

Yes, suffering and pain do not belong to ultimate Reality. God did not create them. We created them.

But God can come into our creations, if we invite Him. That is what prayer is all about. In prayer, we invite God into our suffering hearts. We embrace Her as hope, as solace, as forgiveness.

In this way we feel "the presence." Moving out of darkness into light requires the awareness that light is there. In the downward spiral of self-hatred, light seems to have vanished into a black hole.

When we invite the presence of God, the Holy Spirit, into our lives, we begin to see the eternal light that stands behind the dark images of condemnation which we have placed in our minds. This is the end of the dark night of the soul. In the darkness, we reach for the light. Our healing has begun.

Forgiveness releases us from the past. Swimming in a windswept sea of blame and shame, forgiveness

43

is a life-raft. As soon as we claim it, we know that we are going to be all right.

My life-raft is a simple one. I have made mistakes, and it is okay. I am not my mistakes. I am the one who learns from my mistakes or ignores them. I am the learner or the one who refuses to learn.

I cannot condemn myself for my mistakes. My mistakes are not bad. My mistakes are tools for healing, if I will only have the courage to use them.

Forgiveness is a shift in my perception of what my life is for: I am not being punished. I am being offered an opportunity to grow.

In the moment of self-forgiveness, I know that I hold the key to my own redemption. I do not question that I need to be healed, for I am still in pain. But, unlike before, I now know that healing is possible.

I also understand that no one else can be responsible for my healing. I stop looking to someone else to fix my pain. I know that my pain is a communication to me that something hidden needs to be brought into awareness. Only I can respond to that communication.

On the other hand, my forgiveness also enables me to reach out to others for help. Precisely because I take responsibility for my own healing process, all kinds of help is available to me. I no longer need to be isolated or alone with my pain. I can share my pain. That is part of my healing process.

Just as no one else can be responsible for my healing, so I cannot be responsible for any one else's healing. I can be a friend, a witness, a brother or sister. But I cannot be a healer for someone else. At best I offer a healing relationship.

Any relationship where sharing exists is a healing relationship. All of us need several healing relationships in our lives. We cannot heal ourselves in isolation. We need to share our experiences and support each other in the healing process.

Table A reviews some of the key steps in the self healing/forgiveness process.

Table A
Key Steps in The Process of Healing/Forgiveness

1. First, I recognize that I am not happy and that I want to be happy.
2. Second, I see that my unhappiness is a direct result of my search for happiness outside myself.
3. Third, I see that I inappropriately blame others for my unhappiness, because they have not been able to meet my needs.
4. Fourth, I see that I inappropriately blame myself for having these needs and not knowing how to meet them.
5. Fifth, I see that I can and must take responsibility for healing my wounds if I want to experience joy and happiness in my life.
6. I realize that I am not alone in healing my wounds. By sharing my struggle with others I give and receive the love I need.
7. I begin to see that I have higher purpose and I open to it. I surrender my need to control and invite spirit into my life.
8. I see that the past is over. I put my mistakes behind me by learning from them.
9. I walk free. I forgive myself and everyone around me moment to moment. Thus, I stay in the present, where my joy and happiness is.

Forgiveness is not something we do just once in a while. It is something we do all the time if we want to be free of the weight of the past.

Most of us understand forgiveness only as something that we give to others. That is a misunderstanding of what forgiveness is. When I say "I forgive you" what I really mean is "I forgive myself for taking offense."

We must always begin by forgiving ourselves. Change begins inside our own hearts and minds. Others merely provide us with opportunities to heal ourselves.

~

FALSE FORGIVENESS

False forgiveness is attack in disguise. Sometimes I say to someone who has pushed all my buttons "I forgive you" and what I really mean is "I am angry with you for hurting me. I don't feel that I have the right to be angry at you. So I guess I forgive you."

Anger is not forgiveness. Anger is anger. When you feel anger, it is important to own it, to express it, to work it through. That is an important part of the healing process.

Expressing anger leads to forgiveness. Repressing it prevents forgiveness from happening.

When I express my anger at you, I release it. I then see that my anger is an attack against you. I wanted to attack you years ago, when I felt attacked by you, but I did not. I took offense, I felt anger, but I did not express it. I repressed the anger.

Repressing the anger is a way of pretending that it does not exist. Repressed anger leads to rage.

By expressing anger now I am honest with you and with myself about how I feel. I see my attack against you. Only when I acknowledge that attack can I understand it, or ask you to understand it and not take offense.

False forgiveness doesn't work. It just deepens my rage. It just increases my separation. If anger is felt, it must be acknowledged and expressed.

Accepting our feelings opens the door to forgiveness. This is important for us to understand this.

JUSTIFICATION

Expressing my anger does not justify it. My anger, my hurt, my frustration, etc. can never be justified. These feelings can and must be acknowledged. They cannot be justified.

Justification is a thought about a feeling. It is an interpretation of a feeling. It says "I have a right to be angry because you attacked me."

Acknowledgment, on the other hand, simply recognizes the feeling that is present. It says "Yes, I am angry."

Acknowledgment either leads to the awakening of responsibility or the projection of blame. In the former case, I own my anger: "Yes, I am angry because I feel attacked." I own the "anger" and the "feeling attacked."

47

I do not seek to make you responsible for my feelings, even though your presence in my life helped to bring these feelings to the surface.

The projection of blame denies all responsibility for the feeling. It says: "I am angry and it's your fault."

When anger is projected, we cannot work it through. In order to work it through, we must take responsibility for it. This is not easy, but it is essential to the healing process.

Taking responsibility for what we feel requires the letting go of any justification of the feeling. Accept the "I am angry" part, because that is all you are ready to take responsibility for. Put aside for a moment the "because it's your fault" part, because as long as that is there you can't experience the anger.

Justification is a distancing device. "I'm afraid of my anger so I'll make you responsible for it." This is running away from the feeling.

As you begin to acknowledge the feeling, you begin to take more and more responsibility for it. And so you begin working it through. You are strengthened by your acceptance of your feelings, so you don't feel quite so hurt, or attacked.

Feeling hurt or attacked is the same thing as feeling weak and vulnerable. We feel weak and vulnerable precisely because we have cut off our feelings. When we restore those feelings, we do not feel so weak anymore.

The stronger and more intact I feel, the easier it is for me to let go of the blame. I just don't need it anymore. Then, I can say "I feel attacked by you" rather than "you attacked me." Owning the "feeling attacked" part deepens my healing and my strength.

By the time we have owned the entire feeling, we are able to let it go completely. After all, we only hold onto the feelings we don't acknowledge and own.

Once we accept how we feel, we just go on from there. Nothing else need be done. Even forgiveness is not necessary.

Forgiveness is only necessary to the extent that I continue to hold you responsible for how I feel.

And even then, the person who requires forgiveness is not you. It is myself.

~~

GUILT AND FORGIVENESS

So my goal is acceptance of self and others and my process is forgiving myself when I am unable to do so. My happiness is linked equally to my memory of the goal and my practice of the process.

Forgiveness is always necessary when I have the perception that I failed to love and accept myself or another. Forgiveness allows me to let go of any feelings of inadequacy that arise for me. Forgiving myself is the affirmation that I do not buy into the feelings of inadequacy that invariably arise when I judge myself or another.

Forgiveness keeps the slate of my heart open for Spirit to write on. Spirit cannot communicate with a guilty mind.

Guilt keeps separation alive. Like anger, guilt is a form of attack.

If I feel that I have hurt you and I come to you to apologize, I have done all I can do to make amends. I come to you in humility and say: "Please forgive me. I made a mistake. I have learned from it. I will try not to do it again."

This is a gesture of strength, not of weakness. I come to you as an equal. I do not come to you in shame. I do not come to you in self-righteousness. I come as one who makes mistakes to another who makes mistakes. I trust that you can overlook my mistake even as I can overlook yours.

This is what we ask when we say the Lord's Prayer: "Forgive me my trespasses as I forgive those who trespass against me."

It is a simple gesture, a profound gesture. It is the basis for healing. I must recognize my mistakes if I am to learn from them. But I must also put those mistakes behind me.

I want your forgiveness, but you may not choose to give it. That must not keep me from asking it. I ask it for myself. I make amends for myself. Knowing I have done all I can do to make amends, I can forgive myself, even if you cannot forgive me.

This is the strength of forgiveness. I can always give it to myself, in any situation, provided that I have genuinely offered you the opportunity to join with me in releasing the past.

Forgiving myself cannot be conditional upon your forgiveness of me. It is, however, conditional upon my honesty about the situation and willingness to take responsibility for it.

Once we understand what forgiveness is, we can

understand how guilt masquerades as forgiveness.

Guilt is always contorted. Unlike forgiveness, it never releases me from my pain or feelings of separation.

There are thousands of forms in which guilt appears. For example, I may blame myself because I did not have the courage to ask your forgiveness. Of course, that problem has a simple solution. Unfortunately, the longer I wait to ask for forgiveness, the harder it is to do so. My guilt does nothing for you or for myself. The original hurt remains unhealed.

Guilt may also involve blaming myself because you choose not to forgive me. Your unwillingness to forgive me shows me that you want to hold onto the hurt of the past. You can choose to do that, but you cannot make me responsible for it. If I am ready to heal, I must choose healing even if you don't. All I can do for you is offer love and peace. One day you may be able to accept it.

My guilt seems aimed at myself, but it is also a disguised attack against you. By refusing to forgive myself, I keep you chained to me, even though you are ready to let go.

Guilt is every twisted attempt to prevent forgiveness and healing from taking place.

The guilty appear to be martyrs. They seem to suffer for their sins, yet by so doing only prolong them.

Guilt gets in the way of forgiveness. Feeling guilty is my way of playing games with you and with God. It says: "I know healing is possible, but I choose not to have it now."

Guilt is a distancing device. It keeps me from feeling my anger at you or at myself. In fact, guilt and the denial of anger are psychological twins. They may, indeed, be the same thing.

Beneath all our guilt is a simple feeling of inadequacy. In my guilt I identify with my mistake. Because of that, I can never move beyond it.

That is why the first gesture of healing guilt is to admit the mistake and take responsibility for learning from it. The guilty must understand that they have nothing to gain from self-punishment except more self-punishment.

If we look closely at this self-destructive process, we will see that it rests upon the belief in sin or evil. The belief in our "sinfulness" is one of the hardest beliefs to give up, since the entire edifice of guilt is built upon it. But once this belief is challenged, the whole false construction comes tumbling down.

FEAR VS. SURRENDER

We all have a tendency to want to control our lives. The ego is security based. It wants what is familiar and resists the unknown.

The ego's need to control keeps us from taking risks in our life. Since risk taking is an inevitable part of the learning process, listening to the ego tends to thwart our growth.

Growth comes from encountering new situations, new challenges. It also comes from facing our fears.

Learning and growing is not always a "comfortable" process. We do experience growth pains. This is not because learning is painful, but because we tend to resist the lessons we need to learn.

Pain comes from our resistance. As we begin to embrace the lessons life brings to us, learning happens with greater ease.

The ego wants us to avoid situations which are fearful for us. The ego's attitude is "let the fear win," or "build a defense against the fear." This just postpones our growth.

The door of fear is open to us, but we will not cross the threshold. Why? Is it not because we believe that the fear is stronger than we are? That belief is a self-perpetuating one until we challenge it.

When we walk across the threshold and realize that we are all right, we break the spell. Now we know that we are stronger than our fear. This is a breakthrough understanding.

I am stronger than my fear. I am not my fear. My fear is something that prevents me from being who I am. When I have the courage to be who I am in any situation, fear invariably stands aside.

You can't conquer fear just by understanding this intellectually. You conquer fear by entering into the unknown, by moving in the direction of your growth and seeing that you are safe after all. It is an experiential awareness.

My desire to control my life arises out of fear. My desire to control your life arises out of fear. My need to remember the past or anticipate the future arises out of fear. My need for guarantees arises out of fear. My need to know you will always love me exactly as you do now arises out of fear. Jealousy arises out of fear. Greed arises out of fear.

I do not control my life. Fear controls my life. I seek control but, ironically, I am controlled by the control I seek.

You see, there is no way out of fear other than going through it.

If I run from my fear, it follows me. If I hide from it, it finds me. It knows me all too well, or so I think.

Going through my fear is letting go. It reverses the energy flow.

Letting go means trusting myself, trusting life, trusting God. I have initiated a new phenomenon. I am no longer the victim sitting back and waiting for fear to come and limit me. I am moving through the limits I perceive.

I may be scared, shaking, trembling, but I am moving. I am moving through my belief that fear can control me. I am moving into the space I allowed my fear to take away from me. I am reclaiming that space. It is the space for my growth.

Surrender is a much misunderstood concept. We think surrender means "give control to someone else." That is not surrender. Surrender is recognizing our need to learn and grow, our need to be fully conscious of who we are. We belong to the learning process and it is to that we surrender. We cannot be here and not learn. We cannot be here and not grow. We cannot be here and not begin to walk through our fear. That is the curriculum. It is the universal curriculum.

My surrender is to my learning process. It is to my inner teacher, who helps me go through that process. I do not surrender to another brother or sister. That is preposterous. The guru or guide is within.

Outer teachers may be important to me, but they simply show me what my inner teacher wants me to learn. If they are good teachers, they encourage me to trust and listen within.

I lose touch with my learning process if I project my power onto some external teacher. I learn best from my from my brothers and sisters when I see them as equals. Then learning is sharing, and it is always mutual.

So my surrender is not to specific others, but to my lessons themselves, and to all who would help me learn them. I am responsible for my own learning, but I am never alone in learning. Always there is a brother or sister at my side.

We are here to help each other learn. It is that simple. When we open ourselves to that fact, our relationships become vehicles for healing.

~

SURRENDER TO GOD

My surrender to God is not to someone or something other than me. It is to the deepest, fullest, most inclusive Me. I surrender to the Me which is also You. I surrender to the unity, the wholeness of all creation. I surrender to the Source from which I came.

Surrender to an idea, image, person or persona is not surrender to God. It is the projection of our power outward. It is the belief in idols.

My surrender to God is empowering to me at the deepest level of my being. My surrender to God and my surrender to my true Self are one and the same, for my true Self abides in God, even as I abide in my True Self.

Trusting God means trusting my Self. It is not possible

to trust God and not trust myself, nor vice versa.

Trust is all inclusive. When I trust myself, I trust you and I trust God. That is the Holy Trinity: Self/Other/God. They are One Being expressing as three.

Trusting God means I trust in the innate goodness of all things. I expect a miracle, and so I find one.

I know that I am not, nor can I be, nor do I want to be in control of my life at the ego level. I know that taking control is really losing control. I know it is losing happiness.

I find I'm much happier moving with the spontaneous flow of life. But, once in a while, I start to resist. Fear comes up and my ego tries to take back control again.

And then my pain returns, and I remember that I have a choice. I can let my fear hold me back from my growth or I can move through it trembling. It isn't easy. It's never easy. My hardest lessons are the ones I resist the most. But, when all is said and done, I see those same lessons have also taught me the most.

"The Lord is my shepherd I shall not want." She is always there for me when I need Her. That is the universal experience. I trust in that. I trust in my silent companion, the one who brings me comfort in my pain, guidance in my confusion, hope in my despair, and courage in my fear. To Her I surrender. And in so doing I bow to you, sister. Namaste. I surrender to That One in each of Us.

~~

A SONG OF FORGIVENESS

The snow is falling softly over the marsh, blowing from side to side. Caught in the wind, the pine boughs release their offering. I am there too. I am slipping to the heart. I am slipping down to the heart of love.

Through the sadness, the ennui, the end of personal love, moving into a deepening silence, oblivion of form, into a deep unity, my arms and lips just peculiar shapes of white sadness, forms of fallen flesh whose purpose is now obsolete.

Mine is the sadness of not knowing, sadness of fallen forms. I abide there, here, adrift, like a breath taken or a breath released. I do not know which.

I feel endless.

Form will come and go. It is incidental, like purpose.

And I will come like the snow and cover it over. I will come and make footprints in the snow, footprints that look crisp and clean, though they lie on top of old footprints long covered over.

It has been only a few hours, but it seems now as if it has snowed for days. I watch hypnotically. The part of me that would struggle nods off. I am gliding along the edge, close to sleep. I am the snow. I am the one watching the snow. Watching the snow is like the snow falling.

My body is filling up. Mind is filling up. Snow sits on my lips, sings in my thoughts, spills in my blood. I am the one watching. I am the one falling on all things, bringing myself to all things. I am the one falling.

I am almost without form. I take the form of whomever receives me. I am a quiet prayer, a song remembered for a moment and then forgotten. My body fades from substance to reflection. It is soft, willowy like the snow. It moves through the branches and hands held out to hold it. For an instant, this tiny, wet, ephemeral form is my body. Then it is no longer.

Mind is clearing now. I wipe off the snow and the surface is like a mirror. I see many things, as if for the first time. I am the small animal that tunnels in for the warmth, the child jumping, spinning and rolling, the ecstatic one, creature of this white apocalypse.

"Hey ma, can I go out and play in the snow?" I can hear that voice echo in the space between the white foothills and the lake, but it is with all the other memories, insubstantial, almost forgotten.

Someone died here, but we don't know who it is. The snow leaves no trace of anything having happened. Yet is clear that everyone who has been here has either disappeared, or is disappearing.

"Where do we go when we disappear, Mom? Where do we go?"

I no longer know which way to look, back toward my birth, or forward toward my death. "Where do we Go, Mom? Are you going to disappear, Mom? Are you going to go and leave me here alone?"

I am still a child. I am still mourning the things I do not understand. I am still seven years old and the snow is three feet high. My father is carrying me out to the school bus on Route 3. Where did he go? I got on the bus and waved to him, as the bus sputtered and lunged forward in the snow. Where did he go?

I am just a child. I don't understand these things. My heart is heavy. I don't understand the snow. I don't understand where my footprints go. I don't understand how to recover them.

"Go through the sadness, little one," I say to myself. To me, that child I was will always be little and innocent, like Diedre, who disappeared as suddenly. One day I woke up and she was not there. One day the wind entered her blood and I was robbed forever. And I never forgave.

"Go through the feelings, little one. Feel the pain and the moment of release, the promise of love and its disappointment. Feel it all. There is nothing unworthy of you. It is just the snow falling. It is just the snow falling inside your heart."

"What are snow angels?" my daughter asks.

"Snow angels are our friends," I say. "Snow angels cannot walk. They cannot run. They only fly. And they fly only when the wind blows."

"Is it for real?" you ask. "Is it for real?"

"I don't know, my dear," I say. "I don't know what is real any more and what is not." I don't know.

The snow comes down. It freezes on the branches of the trees. The sun comes out, shines on those frozen shapes, and makes rainbows everywhere you look. I don't know if they are real.

The snow angels come to me at night in my dreams. They sound like galloping ponies as they approach, but as I look carefully I see that their feet never touch the ground. The sound I hear is the gentle flapping of their wings. The sound I hear is the snow falling against my window.

Dear God. I have come full circle. Oh, such sweet sadness, this attachment to form. Must I yet surrender it and leave the ones I love?

I have returned to you clothed only in the windswept snow. I have come through the soft blizzard with tears falling. I have come home, Lord.

~

RECLAIMING THE HURT CHILD

Yes, there is a place in me which radiates divine love. There is a place which is free of judgment, free of fear, free of attack or manipulation. This place is there in every being. It is the primal place, the place of beginnings, the Source place.

Discovering this place of peace and guidance is the most important work of my life. As I find it more and more often, I find that layers of untruth and unreality begin to peel away. I let go of my dishonesty, my need to control others.

I recognize that I want appreciation. I want love. I want to be honored as a unique person. I want to be taken seriously. I recognize that. And I also recognize that my need for all these things has not been satisfied. I have looked for love and support from others, but I have never found it in the way I think I deserve to find it.

I want unconditional love. I will never be satisfied by anything other than unconditional love. This is an honest yearning.

My problem is learning that I cannot demand

unconditional love. If love comes in response to some demand I have made then it is not unconditional. It is coerced. This is the beginning of abuse.

Any demand I make on anyone including myself is abuse!

It is a difficult lesson, but I must learn it. My spiritual growth depends on my learning it. I cannot buy love. I cannot steal it. I cannot appropriate it. If it is love, then it is freely given. If it's not freely given, it's not love.

So I see the writing on the wall. I witness to my own manipulation. I see how I try to get my needs met by others. I see that my search for love, my search for money, my search for recognition is all in vain. "It is all vanity," as the preacher said.

And I realize that there is only one way I can legitimately meet my needs. There is only one way that I can get my needs met without manipulating others. And that is to look within for comfort instead of seeking it through others.

As soon as I stop looking outside of myself for satisfaction, I have to confront my ego head on. It is no longer my ally in the search for outer comfort.

I sit with my ego now. I sit with my fear now. I sit with my scared child now. That is all the ego is: a scared, angry child, trying desperately to protect itself from being hurt. This child has no confidence in me. This child has no confidence in anyone. This child has been hurt, betrayed.

Winning back this child is the most important piece of spiritual work that I will ever do, because when this child has healed, she brings me the gift of trust, the gift of curiosity, the gift of joy. These are the gifts I need. I have been without them for too long. These are the gifts

I sought in vain outside myself. These are the gifts I need to give myself.

I see that I am split. The adult and child need to come back together. That is where the Self begins: in that joining, in that healing. The child is father of the man. Reclaiming the child is the beginning of spirituality.

When I and the child are joined, I feel recognized. I feel loved.

I feel important. My energy is fresh, exuberant. I look forward to each day. I am willing to trust. I don't need to demand and control. I accept what comes my way with gratitude. I enter the flow of the universe.

That is what is means to be "a child of the universe." I am no longer dependent on you per se. I am dependent on all things, and all things are dependent on me. I never fear that because you cannot meet my needs, those needs will not be met. I know that they will be met by myself perhaps, by some friend, or perhaps by a stranger. I do not know how. But I know.

That is the trust of the child. He is here as a guest. He is little and needs help to survive. He is not afraid to reach out. He is not afraid to ask.

We are no different. We are that child. We are God's child. We are God's guest. How can we be afraid to reach out and ask for help?

As I learn to love and accept the inner child, she guides me. She is my true ally, my true support. As the scared, distrustful, unhappy child, she was the voice of ego. Now as the healed, trusting, joyful child, she is the voice of spirit. Before, she was the voice of fear. Now she is the voice of love.

This is the great transformation of my life, the inner

healing and return to who I am.

You see, loving the child is learning to love and accept myself. It is moving from the darkness of fear and separation into the light of love and joining. It is the holy journey.

It is my own journey. I am responsible for it. I am responsible for learning to love myself. I can share my journey with you, but I cannot make you responsible for it. I can receive your love, but I cannot demand it.

Loving myself means recognizing myself. When I recognize who I am, I don't need outer recognition so much. I don't need constant strokes, constant credit. I know I am okay. I know I am good. I know I am beautiful.

That is not Narcissism. Narcissism means that I love myself so much I cannot appreciate you. Narcissism is not self-love; it is self-hate. Is keeps me isolated, unhappy.

My love for myself is the basis for my love for you. My appreciation of myself is the basis for my appreciation of you. Moreover, it is my love for myself which makes it easy for you to love me. I am easy to love when I love myself, because I do not make demands on you.

People who do not love themselves are hard to love. They demand love and so they do not receive it. The affection they receive has strings attached. It is an emotional bargain. It is a business proposition. It has nothing to do with love.

Self recognition makes outer recognition possible. It does not depend on outer recognition, but it facilitates it.

If I recognize myself and share myself with you, you feel affirmed with me. Recognizing me is just a way of embracing something important in yourself.

" When we accept darkness and light together, we move into an awareness of light which is non-physical. This is the light of truth, of compassion, the eternal light."

That is the spirit of help. By helping myself I help you. By loving myself, I love you.

My love for myself is not competitive with my love for you. They are the same love. Loving you never takes anything away from me and vice versa.

Love makes more love. That is the basis for the supply of the universe. Love always makes more love.

All lack is simply a lack of love. Lack of money, lack of recognition, lack of security, lack of trust are all a lack of love. Love is the only cure for scarcity. For where love is, there is no genuine need that goes un-met.

~~

THE ILLUSION OF AUTHORSHIP

When I am insecure about who I am I need to have authorship. I need to be the writer, the teacher, the "creator" of some idea, service or product. I need the role, the definition, the status.

The role gives me legitimacy. It gives me the recognition I so badly want. This is my belief and it is also the belief of many other people who share my insecurity.

As I have lived my life the issue of authorship has come up many times. I have been writing seriously since I was fifteen. The first poem I wrote came from an inner voice. It just flowed through complete. I didn't have to change a word. It was a pure transmission. I heard it and wrote it down.

Then I started to see myself as a poet. The struggle

began. It is not that I stopped hearing the inner voice, but I started trying to manipulate it. I tried to take control. My best poems were the ones that came out whole, with little or no struggle. They were a collaboration between my inner voice and my conscious mind. They were a deep, subtle meaning finding a simple form of expression.

My worst poems were the ones I struggled with for days. I always thought I was writing a great poem, one that others would appreciate. I wanted to be appreciated. I wanted to be successful as a poet. I hid my insecurity under a cloak of sophistication, but it was always there.

In 1973, I was working on a collection of poems entitled "The Thorns of Dawn." I was living in East Cambridge, riding my bicycle three miles to work at 4:00 AM in the freezing cold. I loaded my truck with 50 gallon tanks of hot coffee and pastry carts to deliver to the high rise office buildings in downtown Boston.

Every morning as I crossed the bridge by the Museum of Science I looked at the grim, gray pink sky, and I felt the heaviness of the world in my heart. The sky was grieving. I too was grieving.

As I rode the empty, narrow streets of Beacon Hill, there was a deep peacefulness, but I could not feel it. All I felt was a hollowness inside.

Slowly the city awakened, and people started scurrying about getting to work. I felt like I was in an Escher painting or a Pavlovian experiment: people moving like timid, confused animals, bumping into each other, going to jobs they despised, getting tense, angry at each other for no good reason. The animation of the day was dark and rancid. It was no better than the futility of dawn. Dawn bled. Day was an attack against the soul.

The high point of my day was delivering the coffee and pastry to the little old Jewish women from Chelsea who ran the commissaries on the 10th floor of some mammoth office building. They alone seemed human. Yet they were only making minimum wage. I felt they too were being exploited.

I found no redemption in anything I saw. The outside world was bleak, tawdry, and manipulative. The inside world was a cry for recognition which I feared would never come. I decided that when I finished that book of poems I would take my own life.

Increasingly the imagery of the Book reflected that of the crucifixion. I felt I was witnessing not only my own crucifixion but that of all mankind. It seemed a slow, God-awful death. An all out nuclear war would have been quicker and less painful.

Then one morning I finished the last poem. It was time. I didn't want to kill myself, but I saw no way out. I mentally reviewed my options: slashing my wrists, putting my head in the oven. I was strangely calm and collected. I asked God to give me one good reason why I shouldn't do it (I wasn't sure I believed in God, but I asked anyway). And then I heard a very clear voice telling me to go into the living room and pick up the first book I saw.

I didn't really trust this voice, but it was clear and emphatic, so I decided to see what would happen. I walked into the living room toward the bookshelf and pulled out the first book my eyes lighted on. It was *I and Thou* by Martin Buber.

That book saved my life. I heard every word spoken into my ear as I stood there for hours, transfigured.

That book showed me the way out.

It helped me understand that there are two worlds: the world of suffering (I-It), which I saw all too well, and the world of love (I-Thou), which I only dimly intuited. I saw the world of suffering because that is what I chose to look at. If I were willing to look more deeply, I could see a different world, a world where "the thorns" were removed from the visage of dawn, and Christ brought healed and whole to a place beyond attack.

The roseate skies of morning held hope as well as fear. Which would I choose to see? I could change my life by changing the way I saw it. The presence of love might seem infinitesimally small and retiring, but I had to acknowledge it was there.

When you see only the darkness, admitting the existence of only a tiny ray of light is a turning point. If acknowledged deeply, that ray of light can light up a life in the vice grip of despair.

My way out of darkness was to trust that voice that told me to go into the living room and find that Book. I had been given a lifeline and I needed to trust the one who offered it to me.

From that moment on, my life began to come together. I moved out of East Cambridge to a small basement efficiency near Harvard Square. It was a dingy place, but it was where I wanted to be. Soon thereafter, a Christian Scientist friend of mine introduced me to a man who was editing a magazine and looking for writers. As I put energy out and demonstrated my faith in myself, the external circumstances of my life began to improve.

Seven years later, I came to the end of what had been a fairly stable phase in my life. I decided to get into my

VW van and drive across the country. I was seeking my purpose.

I knew it did not lie in working for others. I knew it was self-directed. I hoped I could find it. I questioned the I Ching and it supported my journey. It told me I would find friends in the Southwest.

While driving across the desert in southwestern Arizona, I received a message to write a book that would be a new system of divination, a synthesis of the I Ching and the Ancient Tarot. All kinds of information about the numerology for the Book began to flow through.

I again questioned the I Ching. Was this guidance reliable? Should I go with it? I received Hexagram I, the Creative. It was clear that I needed to pay attention to what I had received.

I finished the Book in 1982. It was supposed to be published then. I had received an advance. The artist had completed the companion deck containing 81 images. Everything had been set in motion. But the publisher kept extending the publication date.

I knew that he was nervous about the cost of producing the deck of cards. Finally, I told him that if he didn't want to do the book to send it back. He agreed.

I put the Book on the shelf for five years and didn't think about it much. I was puzzled, though. Why had God given me this Book to write if he didn't want it published? You see, I didn't fully trust my own process.

Still, in spite of my insecurity, I was clear about the authorship issue. The material came through me, but it did not belong to me. I was like a midwife. I helped bring it through. My consciousness was essential to the process, but I could not take credit for it. It was His

Book, and He would have it published or not as He saw fit. I needed to let go.

In 1987 I walked into the New Age Bookstore in Hanover, Mass. I went to find a lunar calendar so I could plan meeting times for a healing group I was starting. At the counter, a woman was talking to the owner about healing groups. It was strange. She seemed to be describing my healing group perfectly.

It seemed like a signal from spirit. I felt foolish, but I approached the woman after she left the store. I invited her to come to the healing group. She seemed surprised but said she would call me.

Janaki brought *A Course in Miracles* back to me. I had read it before, but it hadn't sung to me. I had felt that many of the same concepts were present in Taoism, Hinduism, and Buddhism, and I felt more comfortable with them in those contexts. The Christian terminology of the *Course* bothered me.

Janaki had also explored eastern religions. She had been a disciple of Swami Satchitananda for some time. Yet she felt that the *Course* had been able to help her improve the quality of her life in a way that had been missing from her spiritual journey. A strenuous schedule of meditation, yoga, and proper diet had not enabled her to change her tendency to judge other people. The *Course,* on the other hand, had given her a tool that she could immediately use in her life to find the Source of peace within.

I decided to give the *Course* another look. This time when I picked it up, I had the same experience I had had with Martin Buber. In fact, to me, the *Course* was a continuation of "I and Thou."

Janaki also introduced me to Paul Tuttle who was channeling Raj. Raj was expressing Course concepts in simple language. It lacked the poetry of *Helen Schucman's* prose, but it was clearly the same material. Somehow I felt the immediacy of Paul's channeling and I understood that I had been channeling in one form or another since I was fifteen years old! I just had no context for understanding the poems that came through me in "one piece," or the strong inner voice that spoke to me while driving across the Arizona desert.

The next morning I awoke at dawn and went to my study. I sat down in front of a blank sheet of paper, cleared my mind and began writing. The first words were "This is all about authorship." I continued for seven pages without looking back. Then I went back to the beginning to see if what I had written made any sense.

It was clear. It was eloquent.

Later that day, I listened to one of the Raj audio tapes Janaki had lent me. On that tape were words and thoughts almost identical to what I had written.

Was I channeling Jesus? At times when the channeling intensified and speeded up, it seemed that an unmistakable presence was coming through. It had a great energy, an authority like nothing else I had experienced.

I now understand that this presence is available to all of us. Any one can channel Jesus or Holy Spirit if he is willing to open his heart, if he is willing to listen deeply, if he is willing to admit that there is an intelligence that transcends ego consciousness available to him.

Artists and visionaries have always channeled Spirit to some degree. Mystics and healers have felt the presence of Spirit within and helped others be in touch with it. The voice of truth cannot be denied. It is all around us. We are all channels for it. Contemporary scripture is being written all the time. Helen Schucman was certainly one of the great channels of our time. But she is not the only one.

Fortunately for us, Helen always down played her role in bringing the *Course* through. In so doing, she gave us a true gift, for she insured that the *Course* would speak for itself. And clearly it does.

It is essential that we put the authorship issue aside. The voice of truth does not belong exclusively to anyone. It belongs to each one of us equally. Each of us can hear that voice in the silent temple of our hearts, and it is important that we listen there and not to the outer voices that surround us.

For it is in the heart that each of us knows what we need for our growth at any given time in our life. In the heart we know what teachings resonate, and what teachers can help us. We must honor that guidance. Any idea, teaching, teacher, or guide who does not affirm and honor the teaching of our heart takes us away from our purpose.

It is in the heart that we encounter the great teachings of the ages. The words of Jesus, Lao Tzu, or Buddha are not at odds with one another. They are remarkably the same. They have differences of form, not differences of content. They are all forms of the universal curriculum.

As I look around me and see the incredible spiritual work people are doing, I understand that we are all working with the same material. We give it a different emphasis, a different flavor, depending on our consciousness and life experience, but the similarities are extraordinary. It is as if a vast integration is taking place within the collective consciousness. Every field of endeavor is being spiritualized.

We are moving into the new millennium faster than we realize. And each of us is essential to that process. As we hear the voice of Spirit within and follow our bliss, we literally transform the world we live in. Your interests, your talents, your guidance reach to places where I am not drawn to go and vice versa.

We do not need to be concerned with struggles over turf anymore. Each of us has a territory given to us to transform, and that territory is revealed to us as we begin to trust our guidance and take greater responsibility for our lives.

We are all needed. We all have equal access to the voice for God. And it is a significant event when any one of us begins to listen and to share what we hear. For the atonement cannot happen without all of us.

These words come through me, but they are not mine for writing them any more than they are yours for hearing them. To write them, I must hear them first.

To hear I must be silent. In silence, the channel opens and the voice of Spirit flows forth.

When I hear the voice of Spirit, it seems to be my voice. When you hear it, it seems to be yours too. If it is not mine or yours alone, whose is it? Either it belongs to no one, or it belongs equally to all of us!

I was told that the name of the voice I hear is I RECOGNIZE ALL BEING ONE. It is not the voice of an entity, but the voice of truth, the voice for God.

Many beings in and beyond the body speak and hear

this voice. Thus, they extend it. Their personalities hardly matter. For when they come to truth they cease to be separate from one another.

If there is no authorship here, how can there be authorship there? Theirs is a chorus of many voices heard as One. It is the voice for God we hear.

As the preacher says: "There is nothing new under the sun." Knowledge is a gift that is given to me in eternity. I received it then, but forgot I had it. Forgetting I had it, I could not pass it on. But now, dear brother, you remind me of it, and so I receive it and return it to you with love.

~

HARMLESSNESS/DEFENSELESSNESS

In the course of my life, situations occur in which people mis-perceive me and I mis-perceive them. They mistake my intentions and I mistake theirs. In those moments, I lose my peace and joy. They are frustrating moments, but they offer me my best opportunities to learn and grow.

In these moments, I see where I am on the spiritual journey. I see how much I have integrated the principles of love and peace into the mental/emotional fabric of my life.

Every time I am attacked I am offered an opportunity to refuse to take offense, to see my sister's sinlessness and my own. This is difficult terrain, but I can make progress if I am committed to preserving my happiness.

How do I begin? How do I learn not to take offense? Surely it may not happen the first time I try it. I will have

74

to try it many times before I see that I can do it. Many times I will take offense at my brother's attack. Each time, I will see that I am agitated and unhappy. I will know that I have temporarily lost touch with my peace. I will see that in taking offense, I have also given it.

Now I come to the beginning. I recognize that I want peace in this situation. I know that I am responsible for my present happiness. This is the turning point. I stop going forward into pain. Instead, I work backwards to reclaim the peace I lost.

In stepping backward, it is helpful if I stop justifying my angry or hurt feelings, but remain with them so that I can learn what they are really telling me. I remember that "I am never upset for the reason I think" and I let go of my feelings of righteousness around my anger or hurt.

Gradually, I become aware that my anger or hurt is simply telling me that I am disappointed in this situation. I looked to you for love and I received attack. I looked to you for trust and you showed me suspicion. What do I do in the face of this attack? Do I strike back? Do I give tit for tat? That is a simple response. It seems only fair. "An eye for an eye, a tooth for a tooth." Unfortunately, it does not solve my problem, unless a truce is called. Attacking back usually leads to more attack because the assumption behind both attack and counterattack is "I'm right and you are wrong."

What are my other options? Well, I can internalize your attack and repress my anger. I can say: "you're right and I'm wrong. You attacked me so there must be something wrong with me. You responded to me in an unloving way so I must be unlovable." This is what guilt is all about.

This approach rarely works either. By internalizing

your attack I may be giving you the message: "it's all right for you to attack me." Abusive relationships begin with this message from the abused to the abuser.

So the message "I'm right and you're wrong" doesn't restore my peace, nor does the message "You're right and I'm wrong." What then restores my peace?

The answer is simple to understand but difficult to practice. Only love restores my peace. I looked to you for love but you attacked me. There is only one reason why you could have attacked me: you did not feel my love for you. If I want to stop the cycle of hurt, I can do so by offering you the love that you are asking for. In the face of your attack, I can "turn the other cheek."

The other cheek is not stained by bruise or blood. It is whole and pure. I offer you what is whole and pure. Seeing that, how can you attack it?

Offering you love makes me feel good and it makes you feel good. It raises the situation beyond attack, beyond blame.

Will you reject me if I say to you: "Look, we're both upset. We don't see things clearly. Let's stop blaming each other. Let's find a way to love each other right now." Will you feel defensive in the face of this overture? Be honest.

If someone extends to you an olive branch, will you attack him with it? It is not very likely. Attack proceeds from the perception that I am unloved. If you are loving toward me, it is hard for me to reject you, because I want and need the love you offer me.

It is a true release when both people in a conflict can take responsibility for choosing love. But, even if the other person cannot choose love, you still can. Your peace

76

is dependent on the choice you make, not on the one she makes.

So every situation in my life offers me the opportunity to love, regardless of what the other person does. Other people do not create my reality. I do. Once I know that, I don't get off track very often.

LOVE'S PRESENCE

As we move through our internal blockages, it sometimes seems that it is a struggle to love ourselves and others. Love seems to be something *we* must do, something *we* must achieve. We forget that we have a silent companion in this work. We forget that the Father is present in the Son. His nature is love. It is love that conceives the Son.

We are conceived in love. We can actually feel this love if we want to. It is not something abstract. It is not just a theological notion. The Love of God is real and it is present in all of us.

Love abides in us and radiates forth. We need do nothing but be willing to accept ourselves to begin to open to love's presence.

Love is not something that I "do," but something that I "allow" to come forth. Every time I make a demand on myself or you, I block my awareness of love's presence.

The only answer to my ego's striving for control is acceptance and forgiveness. That restores my connection to love.

Love is always there, but I am not always aware of it.

When I forgive myself for my lapse in consciousness, all feelings of separation from love disappear.

I can invite the presence of love within me by:

accepting myself as I am (including my dark side)
accepting you as you are (including your dark side)
forgiving my mistakes (all the forms of attack I engage in)
not being threatened by your mistakes even when you attack
     me,
forgiving myself when I take offense,
asking for help when I need it,
giving help when it is asked of me or I intuit the need for it,
allowing you to take responsibility for your life,
respecting your boundaries and my own, whether real or
     imagined, so that we cannot use them to separate us,
being patient with myself,
being patient with you,
being patient with God,
seeing God in your face,
seeing God in my own face,
seeing God in everything that happens in my life,
taking responsibility for everything I am creating here and
     now.

These positive actions call love forth from deep inside me. They unite me with my Source and help me live my life in the flow of grace.

REVELATION

A Course in Miracles says God takes the last step. All S/he needs is a little willingness on our part. What is that willingness?

It is the willingness to let go of the fear. Letting go of the fear is the invitation to love.

It is the willingness to relinquish our suffering. Relinquishing our suffering welcomes our joy.

It is the willingness to move through our doubt. Moving through our doubt is a call to faith.

It is the willingness let go of judgment. Letting go of judgment helps us see our sinlessness.

When we remove what is not there, we see what is there. Our job is to remove the illusions we have made. God's job is to reveal to us the Reality behind them.

We can work hard at undoing what we have made, but let us not forget what we did not make. Let us experience that as well. If we do not take time to feel love's presence in our hearts, the process of moving through our pain is a grim one.

As we open our hearts to one another, there is a warmth that comes and goes. It is not dependent on any particular relationship. It comes whenever we are being accepting of ourselves and of others. When it comes we feel grateful. When it goes we look for it to return. And so we begin to welcome it and value it more deeply.

The form of our relationships becomes not so important as the feeling of this presence in each and every one.

When it is there, we know the relationship is holy. When it is not, we know there is healing necessary.

Devoting myself to healing all my relationships brings the presence deeply into my life. It is there in all that I do, guiding me. I move from its warmth, and others feel that warmth in my attention, my concern, my touch. Love's presence blesses me and all that I do.

There is no real mystery in this. I feel loved, so I can give it gladly. I am not Love's architect, but its minister. I am not the giver of life, but the channel in which life flows. As it flows through me, it extends to you, brother. It touches you sister. And I am touched in turn by the way you channel love to me.

In giving, I am in touch with the giver of life. In receiving, I accept the fact that Love is my nature. For I can only receive what I am. I can only receive love if I am love. And I can only give love if I have acknowledged it in myself.

OPENING THE WAY OF THE HEART

Feeling love's presence in my life and hearing the inner voice are one and the same. They only appear to be different.

Love's presence is felt in the heart. The inner voice is heard in the mind.

What is the mind but the shape the heart takes? An open heart is an open mind. A closed heart is a closed mind.

The heart feels all things. The heart does not judge. It

feels. There is no end to its feeling. It feels me. It feels you. It feels the world. It feels what is beyond the world.

The heart feels all things. It feels pain. It feels fear. It feels joy and bliss. There is nothing it does not feel.

What the heart feels shapes the mind. Feeling fear is a contraction of the heart. Feeling joy is an opening.

As the heart opens, so does the mind. As I feel love's presence, I begin to hear my guidance.

Trying to hear my guidance without opening my heart is not possible. Guidance comes from love, not from fear.

If my heart is contracted, I cannot be in touch with my guidance. I must be willing to trust just a little bit. I must be willing to relax just a little bit.

I must be willing to surrender, to let go, to let God. That is why our most profound revelations happen through emotional catharsis.

A tight heart cannot hear the word of God.

Spirituality happens from the inside out. If I want to meet God, I must go inside. I must descend into Hades, into the dark world of my emotions. I must wrestle with my shadow, as Jacob wrestled with the angel, as Job wrestled with his concept of a vengeful God.

I must redeem the lost self, the hidden self, the self denied. I must heal the split inside myself. I must face my darkness if I would see the light.

I cannot feel joy if I do not face my sadness. I cannot feel love if I do not face my fear. Changes in thinking happen when we change the way we feel, not the other way around.

That is why I call my work "Opening the Way of the Heart." The heart feels all things and it is in the heart that our work of integration begins.

THE ATONEMENT

I do not want to be embroiled in controversy. I do not want to take sides supporting one brother or sister against another. I do not want to make someone right, including myself, if it makes another wrong. I do not want to make myself wrong either.

I want to respect all beings, including myself. And the only way I can do that is to admit my mistakes.

Why do I admit my mistakes? Because I need to come to a genuine honesty about who I am. I need to realize that I am not my mistakes. Admitting my mistakes helps me release them. Not admitting them is a way of holding onto them.

When I admit my mistakes, I learn from them. Indeed, I cannot admit my mistakes to you unless I have first admitted them to myself and I am willing to embrace the lessons behind them. When I share my mistakes with you, I am acting as a learner, not as a wrong-doer.

As I wrong-doer I condemn myself and you. As a learner, I embrace myself and you. We are all learners. We are equals.

In my Course support group, there are frequent tensions and ego struggles between us. Our group is not some model to the world of people living the Course. Our group is a microcosm of the world. Ego arising in each one of us in the group is the same ego arising in us at home or in our workplace.

We bring our egos to the group. We intend to place

them to the side so that we can hear the voice of Spirit, so that we can create a listening and accepting atmosphere for each other. But it does not always work.

Each of us struggles with the group. Each of us goes through times when the group does not seem to be meeting our needs. And we want to pull back. We want to stop coming. This is the hurt child — the voice of ego — telling us our needs aren't met so we'd better defend ourselves or run away from the conflict.

Yet each of us also hears a different voice. It is the voice of Spirit telling us "everything is okay," telling us "you're only upset because you are trying to take control. You are trying to manipulate the group to meet your needs, just as you have done with every group you have ever belonged to since you were a child. You are still a child. You are still trying to take control, because you hurt, and you want, and what comes back from others is not medicine for your deepest wounds."

The group is just a microcosm of our lives. I don't want to be in ego in my group, so I try to show only the side of me that seems resolved. I hide my dark side and turn up my lights. In the face of those bright high beams, who can tell that there is an aggressive, impatient, dark blob trailing?

Who can tell? Well, just about everyone can tell except myself! That's because one ego knows how to spot another one. When I am attacking, everyone in the group feels attacked. Now we are all in ego. We are all struggling.

If we ever needed to practice the Forgiveness, It Is In our Course group. Here we are ostensibly talking about Spiritual principles, and before two words have been said, we're enmeshed in the ego experience. It is ironic.

We all bring our lessons with us. We all bring our darkness, whether we would admit it or not.

So, rather than realize that the Spirit has the group exactly where S/he wants it, we try to take control of it. We try to make the group fit our needs. We seek the agreement of others in the group so that we can move the group in a direction that is less threatening to us. We polarize. We take sides. We attack, defend, feel hurt and run away from each other.

"Who needs this?" we all say in our private hearts. "I get this all day. I don't come to this group to be in ego. I might as well not come. Who needs more suffering? Who needs more conflict? I already have enough of that in my life. I think I'll just stop coming to the group."

All of us have gone through this internal scenario. We all want to run, but somehow we stay together. There is something here that we need. We don't know exactly what it is, but we sense its presence.

This something is simply the truth we have all come to hear. It is the voice for God that dwells equally in each one of us. We don't hear that voice when we are in ego, nor do we hear it when we are punishing ourselves or others for being in ego.

We hear that voice only when we let the attack go, when we no longer have an agenda for the group, but simply allow it to be. We hear it when we stay in the moment, listening to our brother, or realizing that we have stopped listening and then bringing our attention back so that we can join again. When our brother speaks, we have a simple choice. We can join him or attack him.

Listening to our sister is joining. Not listening to her is attacking.

Responding to the issues or concerns my brother raises is tricky business. Am I taking issue with him, or simply sharing my own experience? There is a big difference. I don't have the right to question my brother's experience, even if it differs from my own. Those differences are holy, if I would just let them be.

We can each have our experiences. We can each have our beliefs. We can each have our unique understanding of *A Course in Miracles,* or our unique struggle with it. Certainly what I understand is no more or less valuable than what you understand.

We are here as equals. We are all teachers for each other. We are all students of each other. Spirit speaks and listens through each of us.

I cannot coerce my sister into sharing if she is not ready. I can simply make my own witness and listen for hers. I must not judge her because she is ripening. I need to be patient and let the fruit fall from the vine when it is ready. I leave that to the Holy Spirit. It is not my affair.

If I make it my affair, I am intruding on Spirit's function. I am contradicting my invitation to Him/Her to be present here.

The *Course* is not about staying out of ego. The concept of staying out of ego is an ego concept. It divides me from my Self.

It is far easier to admit that I am in ego and I would like not to be. I do feel separated and I would like to feel connected. That is a more honest appraisal of where I am. From this place I can operate with integrity. I don't have to measure up to some kind of false image of myself that others all too readily see through.

Once I have let this false image of myself fall away, it

is easier for you to do the same. If I'm not pretending to be holy, you don't feel attacked by my "holiness" and you don't have to defend yourself by putting on airs of "holiness" too.

Can there be any doubt of what's behind the attitude: "I'm holier than you are." Let's face it, the ego is just an insecure child. He is so insecure, he needs to keep telling you: "My understanding is more profound than yours."

When the child feels inadequate, she'll try anything to try to make herself feel whole. Unfortunately, she cannot heal herself by attacking others.

So where do we begin the healing process in our classes and support groups? I believe that we begin by admitting our imperfection, by admitting our tendency to be in ego most of the time.

My spiritual "perfection" lies in admitting my human "imperfection." Pretending to be "perfect" is a heavy burden and an unnecessary one. Pretending to be joyful, thankful, and loving when we don't feel that way is not spirituality; it's self-deception.

My self-deception sets me up for failure. When I see myself as perfect, discovering my imperfection is a tremendous disappointment. I feel as unworthy as I once felt proud. Psychologically, I crash. The distance is too great between who I am and who I'm pretending to be.

It is always easier to see this in others than it is to see this in myself. I can spot "un-groundedness" and "wish fulfillment spirituality" from miles away, but I cannot see it as it arises in myself. I can spot others puffing themselves up, but I hardly recognize my own version until I hear myself saying "I'll huff and I'll puff and I'll blow your house down."

What I begin to realize though, is that it is a tremendous relief to me to be honest about who I am. When my self image and my feelings about myself are not greatly at odds, I am more comfortable with myself, and I am also more comfortable with you.

It also makes it easier for me to understand and accept that being in ego and learning from it IS my spiritual process. It IS my path. I don't have to dread the moments when I huff and puff. I don't have to hide them, disguise them, run away from you so you won't see them.

When I accept my imperfection, I don't have an image to protect. Who needs to protect imperfection? It's already imperfect. There's nothing you can add to it to make it more imperfect.

Accepting my imperfection means making room for all of myself. It brings forgiveness with it. It means surrender to who I am at a deeper level than that one at which I judge myself or you.

Deep within my acceptance of my imperfection is a bottom line affirmation of who I am. Deep within it is an existential and complete sense of adequacy. This Self affirmation is simple and pure. It is not done at your expense, for it is not competitive with you.

As I "get real" with who I am, it takes nothing away from you. It just invites you in, without judgment. It welcomes you without expectation.

When I am Real, I don't depend on you to uphold or confirm my "reality." If you don't buy it, it's okay. That doesn't take it away from me, because I am used to standing alone with it. Your lack of support for me cannot make me feel inadequate, because my sense of adequacy is bottom line. It comes from deep within me. It is my decision to live and not to die. I am no longer struggling with my imperfection. I have embraced it.

I am here not to pretend that "attack is not real" but to own the attack. I am here not to pretend that "pain doesn't exist" but to own the pain. I am here not to pretend that "I'm not in ego" but to own my egotistical thoughts and actions. That I can do.

Owning my attachment to unreality deepens my reality, because it ends the separation between what I accept and what I refuse to accept about myself.

Non-dualistic perception, which the *Course* calls Knowledge, is total. It is not partial. I do not accept one brother or sister at another's expense. I accept all or none. I do not accept part of myself at the expense of some other part. I accept all or none.

Now we approach the meaning of the at-one-ment. To be at one with myself, I must accept all of myself. To be at one with my brother or sister, I must accept all my brothers and sisters.

I cannot be partially saved, nor can I be saved alone. As long as there is one brother or sister in ego, peace is not total. The world still abides, with its conflicts, its treachery, its elaborate systems of defense.

When I am in ego, I threaten your peace. When you are in ego, you threaten mine. Sure, I would like my peace to be independent of your thoughts or actions, yet I also see that we have chosen to be here together. I have chosen to share my peace, not to have it separately.

My salvation has to do with something larger than my self affirmation. My salvation begins with my self-affirmation, but does not end with it. What I affirm in me must extend to all before it is complete. This is what it means to return home.

When we are all at peace, Heaven is on earth. We live by heaven's laws. There is no attack, because there is no longer any defense.

So my *Course* group is a microcosm of the world. I am not saved alone. I do not meet my needs by opposing the needs of others. We are all here together. We come to listen and to support. Sometimes we are unable to hear. Sometimes fear arises and we attack. Sometimes impatience arises and we try to push each other along. It doesn't work. We are unhappy.

We want to leave the group, but we can't. We can't because our purpose is here. We can't because our purpose is to forgive. Only forgiveness works. Only forgiveness opens the hearts that fear has closed.

THE ILLUSION OF LEVELS

In my teaching, sometimes I give the impression that I have all my issues resolved. It isn't true, but because of the role I'm playing people sometimes buy Into thIs perception. I sometimes buy into this perception myself.

I didn't start teaching because I had become "enlightened" and wanted to impart my enlightenment to others. I started teaching because that is what I really enjoy doing. I love to share what I am learning. Sharing it helps me learn it even more deeply.

It is easy for us to become attached to the role of "teacher." Often, the person who has read the most books becomes the authority figure in a group. While this may be comforting for the group initially, it is a fatal mistake to make anyone in the group special. If all participants are not equal, the basis for growth is compromised.

Our proficiency with *A Course in Miracles* is not measured by how much we have read, but on how much we have understood and integrated in our daily lives. One who understands the truth does not "teach" it. She models it. She gently defers to others and helps them hear the truth within their own hearts.

In my experience, spiritual growth is not a linear, left brain, achievement-oriented activity. Indeed, it requires our willingness to move into the unknown with trust and faith. If you are an "expert," you think you already have the answers. So you can't make space for the truth to emerge spontaneously in the moment.

In our group, we are all equal, no matter how long we have been studying the *Course*. We all have something to share.

My decision to do the lessons for the four hundredth time does not give me a special dispensation on *Course* understanding. A new student approaching the lessons for the first time may open my eyes to meanings I could not glean before.

We must be careful not to become attached to the form of our spirituality. People running around quoting blue and gold books are no more sensitive or endearing than other missionaries who knock on our doors to "save us" from ourselves. Like all great scriptures, the written *Course* gives way to the unwritten *Course*. Form gives way to content. We must not worship the package, but the gift it encloses.

At the conclusion of the *Course,* Jesus, releases us to

the Holy Spirit, from whom he learned. Jesus taught us to open the Channel. Now we must listen to the voice that comes through it.

Jesus is not the voice for God, but the one who hears it. In hearing it, he joins with it. In joining with us, he brings it to us. He has led us to the clear stream. Now we must drink.

Every one of us is a sleeping Christ. Like Moses, each one of us receives the tablets of the law. The Sermon on the Mount, the tablets of the law received at Sinai were once contemporary revelation, contemporary scripture. The *Course* is contemporary scripture. All around us, Spirit is speaking. The voice for God is as alive now as it was two thousand years ago. To him who hungers will water be given. To she who knocks, will the door be opened.

None of us is special. Or all of us are. But some of us are not more or less special than others.

Today I am the teacher, yet tomorrow you will teach me. It does not help me to cling to the role of teacher, for in so doing I cease to learn. When I can recognize the voice for God coming from your lips, I can surrender my need to control and give my learning process back to God.

It is as blessed to follow as it is to lead. Those who stand back will come forward, and those ahead will stand aside and make room for them. "For each thing, there is a time and purpose under heaven." That is the Tao. That is God's plan at work.

And so I pray: "Lord guide me. Thy will be done in me and through me. Be in charge of my comings and goings. Let me not be afraid when you ask me to lead

91

and to speak. Let me not be attached when you ask me to listen and surrender. In all that happens, allow me to re-cognize that you are with me. In my strength are you present. In my gentleness are you present. Allow me to meet the need that arises before me that my needs may also be met without conditions.

What level do I occupy? Do I stand at the top of the stairs or at the bottom? Will I stand aside and let you pass, or shall I run to catch up with you? You see, it is all a game of circles. I am not further along than you, nor am I behind you.

You and I stand side by side, brother. We stand together. What can be said about you can also be said about me.

We keep trying to shed our equality, but we cannot do so. It is a condition of who we are. It goes wherever we do.

This alone I know: that I am equal to you and that you are equal to me. Everything else I may call into question, but not this. For upon this does my true identity rest.

Being gentle with my sister is the best way for me to love myself. I can look for other solutions to my problems, but I will never find as good a one as this. Being gentle with my sister is the best way for me to love myself.

Yes, I know that you are with me, God, but I do not know the form your message will take. I do not know if it will come through my lips or through my brother's. And when it comes, I do not know if I will open my heart to it or if I will try to push it away. Will I claim my power, or project my imperfection? Will I strike out at my sister or claim sanctuary in her loving arms?

I do not know. I know only that you are with me.

"No one can forgive you except you. That is why it is your first act of courage, your first act of love. Everything positive in your life stems from this simple but often profoundly difficult act."

And that whatever I do or neglect to do, I can turn to you and see my innocence reflected.

That is your gift to me. You have given me the freedom to make mistakes and learn from them. You have let me have my problem so I could find the solution. You did not force your love upon me, but let me come to you when I was ready. For this, I thank you, Lord. You have been patient with me. May I be as patient with my brother and sister as you have been with me.

~

THE ATTACHMENT TO SUFFERING

As our awareness moves to the heart, we find that we are able to reach out more genuinely to our brother and sister. Accepting and sharing our feelings establishes a bond with others and heals our sense of separation.

Our feelings are indeed the doorways to truth and healing when we have the courage to move through them. Moving "through" them, however, means that we eventually go beyond them.

Sharing my pain is generally helpful. It creates emotional movement for me that ultimately culminates in my letting the pain go. I move through my pain so that I can reclaim my peace.

If peace is not the outcome of being with my feelings, then I may be attached to those feelings and unable to let them go. Perhaps staying with my feelings when I am ready to move through them is a way I have of gaining attention from others.

Others do tend to focus on me when I am in pain, when I am sick, when I am apparently vulnerable. Perhaps I find that this is the only way I have to get people to pay attention to me. So I may not want to give up my pain or my illness.

This attachment to my pain is as counterproductive to my spiritual growth as is its opposite: denial of pain. Denial keeps me from experiencing my feelings. Attachment keeps me from letting them go when I am ready.

The healing process is two fold. It involves both letting in and letting go, recognition and release.

Pretending that the pain is not there is not helpful to me, nor is preoccupation with the pain. Both are forms of addiction. Both increase my separation from myself and others.

If I don't acknowledge my pain, I can't begin the journey out of it. I can't take responsibility for my pain. I can't let you know I hurt, because I fear the intimacy involved in sharing this. I can't open my heart. I can't reach out to you. I can't move through my pain.

On the other hand, if I latch onto my pain, then I make my healing your responsibility instead of mine. I run the risk of alienating you by holding onto you too tightly. You may begin feeling guilty when I don't get well because you have bought into my mistaken belief that you are responsible for my healing.

Both the refusal to feel and the attachment to feelings represent an inability to take responsibility for my feelings. Both attitudes short-circuit the healing process.

I am responsible for what I feel, not you, not God. I am the one who feels this way. No justification is necessary. Justification just gives me an excuse to hold onto the feeling. My goal is not to hold onto pain, but to move toward peace. Being with my feelings is a kind of prayer for love, for all of my feelings are a cry for love.

When I listen to my feelings, I hear myself calling for love. I hear the cry of the child within. And hearing it, I begin to honor it. Listening brings love. Trusting brings movement.

Before I learned to listen, the child was frantic. He screamed but I could not hear him. Toward the end, he stopped screaming. He became mute, lifeless. He began to pull me into his despair. I could feel the downward, tornado-like swirling, the movement into the black vortex of anger and fear.

He made sure that I paid attention. He made sure that I healed the separateness between him and me.

This scenario will be familiar to anyone who has had trouble coming to grips with feelings. The longer I repress how I feel, the more intense the process of reconnection becomes.

The same is true when I project the responsibility for my feelings onto others. I make my well-being dependent on how others behave toward me. I hold them hostage. I get sick and they feel responsible. A tumor grows inside me. It is my tumor, my attack on myself, but they feel responsible for it.

I am convinced that only they can heal me. But they cannot. I demand their love, but I feel betrayed. In their guilt and helplessness they move away from me, denying me the one thing I thought I could control. Now I am alone with my illness. I am alone with my pain. And now, if I can let go of blame, now if I am really ready to take responsibility, my healing can begin.

People who are responsible for their feelings do not punish themselves. They do not punish others. They move from dis-ease to ease, from pain to peace. They heal and their healing is a testament to the power of truth. All who see it are empowered by it. For when one of us is healed, all of us are lifted up.

THE TRANSMISSION OF THE HEART

In 1975, I met a woman who was to have great impact on my life. When I was with her, I felt a powerful burning sensation in my heart center. Energy flowed between us and seemed to bathe our entire bodies in its embrace.

Sometimes this would happen when we were lying down together, holding each other. Other times, it would happen as we were sitting together at a concert, holding hands. Often, it would happen in some nonchalant moment when our eyes met.

I surrendered with her, as she did with me. Love held us holy and we rested there together. I experienced great peace, great comfort. It was my first experience of giving and receiving unconditional love.

Whenever I see Judy, even if I have not seen her for years, the same feelings of connection, the same warmth, the same acceptance of her and of myself with her arise for me. It has nothing to do with time or space. It has nothing to do with the roles that we play in our lives. It is not based on agreement of beliefs or sexual attraction. It goes beyond all that.

I did not understand what this was for some time. It seemed an un-repeatable experience. Yet as my own spiritual practice unfolded and I found myself opening up, I began to feel the same burning sensation in my heart center whenever I felt deeply accepting and vulnerable with another human being.

Now this sensation is with me continuously. Whenever I listen deeply, whenever I let go of judgment and accept another or myself, whenever I share something or witness to someone else's sharing, the ecstatic warmth is there.

It took a long time for me to recognize that the path of the heart was my path. Now that I have embraced it, I can look back at my life and see that it all fits. The loving embrace of my grandfather Isaac whose eyes met mine at two or three years old in the depth of my soul. We rarely spoke, but I knew his love without doubt. The moments as a teen-ager in my uncle Vincent's shack, listening to him and knowing what he would say before he said it. The feelings of deep connection with other beings. The intimacy that seemed to transcend space and time. The growing connection to God. The opening up to the inner voice.

It has all been a process of opening my heart. As a child I was very open and absorbed a great deal of negativity. I closed down fairly early. The first twenty years of my life were a struggle with that negativity and the defense mechanisms I had built against it. I had lots of anger, often rage, which got expressed in my first few adult relationships. I had to go through the dark tunnel toward the light. It wasn't easy.

At first I blamed my parents. My father was distant,

but safe. My mother was close, but emotionally controlling. I was an emotional refugee looking for love and safety in the same package. I couldn't find it.

When I started to take responsibility for my relationship with my parents, my healing process began. It has been a long, steady process. Today, I feel close to both of my parents. They have both grown in their lives. I have respect for their journeys. I have come to love and appreciate them as people.

When the heart is closed, it is not easy to open. Behind those closed doors are powerful feelings, many of them negative. Understandably we are afraid to release the tide. We imagine it will be blood red. We are convinced there will be casualties.

In reality, I am the only casualty of my emotional life. I am the one who closed down. My defenses cut me off from others. I felt miserable. I couldn't begin to heal until I admitted that I felt miserable.

For me, pain has been a journey toward bliss. Darkness has been a journey toward the light.

Where there was fear and suspicion, there is now warmth and acceptance, not always, but much of the time. I feel good about myself now. I love myself now.

It is my journey through the darkness that enables me to reach out to others in pain. Had I not been there, I could not help. My ability to help comes equally from my compassion for the pain others feel and my feeling of being loved. Because I am loved, I hold the light up to the dark places.

I am not afraid of the dark, hidden place, the cave of the ego, for I have been there. I can enter there with a tiny taper. I can lead the way to where the light comes in by itself. Then I must leave you at the entrance to the cave. I must let you turn back toward the darkness or go forward toward the light. It is your choice.

It is God's will that it be your choice. The messengers of God see the light and so bring it to their brothers. I see the light in you and I tell you of it. But you must see it too. You must claim it.

The transmission of the heart is a simple one. It does not have to speak in words. It comes as pure feeling. It translates in a look, a touch, a smile of encouragement. It says: "you are my sister, like to me in every way. I see the light in you, even as I see it in myself. You are totally acceptable. You are totally loved. I am the one who brings this message, but it comes not from me. The One who knows you best loves you best. S/he accepts you just as you are. Be still and know this. Be still, my sister, for the peace of God dwells in your heart.

~

BROTHERHOOD/SISTERHOOD

Sean was a student in my Tarot class in Boston in 1978. He would always answer questions at a different level from most of the students. That was interesting.

But what was even more interesting was that I kept running into him in Harvard Square. At first it seemed a coincidence. But then it seemed that, without planning to, I would be seeing him every day.

We became friends. It was clear before too long that Sean was my teacher too. Whenever I needed a boost in my journey, he always had it to give. Many important books have come to me through Sean, and always at the right time. He was my spiritual lending library.

Sean had been a follower of Bubba Free John, but had decided to go the journey alone. Both of us wanted to belong to a spiritual community. We wanted the guidance of a master. But we just couldn't find one teaching or teacher who spoke to us. It was the loneliness of the journey that was difficult for both of us. In our friendship, we found community.

We came together and let each other go. We had great respect for each other's path. We learned from each other.

In spite of the fact that we shared intellectually, it was Sean's tremendous heart-centered energy that helped me the most. It wasn't just me. Whenever any of my friends met Sean, they felt an instantaneous connection. In Sean's presence, people felt loved and accepted. It was a phenomenal thing.

Yet I knew that Sean was lonely in the same way I was. He never saw the tremendous positive impact he had on others. He was looking for more than human affection. He was seeking enlightenment. He was seeking the Self.

Sean came to me as a student, yet he has been my best teacher. We are brothers. Our journeys are different yet the same. We know that. We come together and go apart. Sometimes we bring great insight and solace to one another. Sometimes neither one of us can penetrate the other's sadness.

That is really the way it is in all of my relationships with my brothers and sisters, regardless of their appearance or the role expectations attached to them.

Sometimes we connect deeply and sometimes we don't.

Our relationships are not defined by the roles we play in relation to each other, nor by where we live or how often we see each other. We may live together and rarely open to one another. Or we may live at a distance and open deeply when we connect.

You and I are on different journeys, yet our journey is the same.

You may have a different religious tradition, yet I might feel closer to you than I do to those who share my tradition. You may share my beliefs, yet I might feel cut off from you.

We are all in different places until we meet in the heart. If we meet and do not understand one another, have we met at all?

We cannot judge each other by the clothes we wear. My beliefs are just a different set of clothes from the ones I wear on my body. They are not that much more profound.

I am not my beliefs and you are not yours. Our relationship is not based on the agreement of our minds, but on the agreement of our hearts.

When we agree in our hearts, I accept you and you accept me. That is real joining. Sharing ideas and concepts may help in that joining or it may prevent it from happening. If I am in my head when I approach you, I cannot touch your heart. If I am in my heart, I feel love for you whether or not my ego is interested in what you say.

The ego builds alliances with people. It seeks out people who share its beliefs so that it can stand strong against the beliefs it opposes. Alliances of mind are not as strong as those of the heart. The alliances of the heart are based on love. You are in my family. Even if you do something I do not approve, you are still connected to me and I will defend you, not because you are right, but because I love you.

We all belong to the same family, but we don't know it. Every time we look for agreement, we separate. Seeking the same ideas, the same race, the same sex, the same religion, we inevitably find what does not fit. What does not fit takes us into the heart.

Accepting what does not fit means looking beyond appearances. It means finding each other at a different level. If you are black and I am white, our egos will use our differences to separate from each other. But if we are together long enough to get through our fear of each other, our bonding will be deeper than it might have been with someone similar to us. That is because it is not based on common experiences and ideas, but on our humanity and our sinlessness.

We are different from each other in many ways, but all those differences are superficial ones. Those differences are maybe ten percent of what we are. They are the tip of the iceberg. Beneath the tip, our similarities run deep. Ninety percent of what we are is shared and we can only feel it in the heart.

The ego sees only the tip of the iceberg. It is aware of every one of our differences. It analyzes them and keeps track of them. It contrives intricate justifications for why these differences must keep us separate.

But it is all in vain. In our hearts, we know we are related. The heart "recognizes all being one." That is why resting in the heart and quieting the ego are one and the same thing.

Sean is my teacher and I am his. We do not hold each other hostage to what we share. We let go. Each of us moves to embody his own journey. Our separation is gentle. Being gentle, it brings us face to face when we are ready to share.

The I Ching says that one must know "when to separate and when to unite." That is what a Holy Relationship is all about. When I let you go, you seek me when you are ready. Then our meeting has significance, because we both surrender to it.

Coercion of any kind in our relationships is forced joining. Forced joining will not permit separation. It does not tolerate differences. And so it can never truly unite us.

Only what I set free has meaning. If I acknowledge my differences with you and give us both the space we need to grow, then our joining deepens, because it is built on trust.

In such a relationship, we are equals. In it, there is both freedom and commitment. Those are the qualities that are present in my relationship with God and, the more I value that relationship, the more those principles become embodied in my relationship with you.

VULNERABILITY

Being in the heart we are always vulnerable. We are always within arm's reach. It would seem that we would be easy targets for attack, for we have chosen to be accessible to one another. Fortunately, this is not so. Our vulnerability actually protects us from attack. Ironically, it is our defensiveness, our chronic sense of separation from one another, that makes us easy targets.

When I was fifteen, I was asked by my best friend to talk to her sister who was depressed. The sister was sitting by herself, sobbing in the front seat of her car. I knocked on the window and asked her if she wanted to talk. She did.

We had a good talk. I think it was helpful. As we were finishing, there was a knock on my window. A voice said: "Get out." I did.

Before I knew what was happening, I was hit by a vicious punch. It knocked me back about two or three feet. I did not understand what was happening. I did not feel anger. I was being attacked, but I did not feel defensive. I knew that I had done nothing wrong. I had no desire to fight this person. The only desire I had was to find out why he was attacking me.

I took several more punches while I tried to speak to him and ask him what the problem was. Then, others intervened.

Vincent turned and walked away in shame. I felt dazed. I still did not understand.

Later, I found out that Vincent had gone out with my friend's sister and felt possessive of her. She had little interest in him, but he would not leave her alone. Apparently, when he saw me sitting in the car with the woman he wanted, he thought I was taking her away from him.

Nothing could have been further from the truth. Vincent's false perception of the situation led to his attack on me. Apparently, I was not the first person he had attacked. I heard stories of many fist fights he had initiated, often without cause. He had a reputation for being a hothead and a difficult person to be around.

Later, Vincent apologized to me. I don't know if he did it because he felt pressured by my friends, or whether he felt genuine remorse. I would like to think it was the latter, but I suppose it doesn't matter. I felt sorry for him. He had a difficult family situation. He felt very alone. He did not know how to deal with conflict in his relationships. He probably thought that others were judging him, so he attacked them. It had become a pattern he just could not get out of.

Like me, many of those people he attacked were probably neutral about Vincent, at least until they were attacked by him. Thus, Vincent's feeling about being judged and excluded by others became a self-fulfilling prophecy.

For me, the incident brought into crystal clarity my understanding that I did not want to fight with my brother. I understood that the whole basis for attack was mis-perception, and the way to undo attack was to undo the mis-perception.

A similar incident happened in grade school, but I

"We must always begin by forgiving ourselves. Change begins inside our own hearts and minds. Others merely provide us with opportunities to heal ourselves."

had no basis for understanding it. There was a boy who took an instant dislike to me, or so it seemed. He used to wait for me after school and taunt me, calling me Jewboy and waving his fists at me. I could never understand what he had against me. I tried to walk home a different way to avoid him. Sometimes it worked. Sometimes it didn't.

In the end, he just went away. He must have found a better target for his anger. Taunting me must have been boring after a while. I just kept walking.

Why did he choose me? Why did I choose him?

Looking back, I can see that on some level I felt guilty. He called me Jewboy and I was half Jewish. Of course, he had no way of knowing that, since my last name was Italian and I never told anyone I was half Jewish.

It wasn't the first time I had been called Jewboy. For years I had been taunted by schoolmates, and I think I had begun to feel that there was something wrong about being Jewish. There was nothing personal in these attacks, but I took them personally.

Back then I did not know about racism. I just knew that people did not like me "because I was Jewish." That just made me hide my Jewishness more. I could never stand up and be proud of what I was, because in so doing, I would lose the affection of my peers, or so I thought.

In my capitulation I became a target for aggression. It was a theme that ran through my early life. The junior high school I went to was ninety percent black. Every day in the corridors I would be verbally abused and threatened by black students. One day I was actually threatened by a six foot black girl who had a knife.

Here I was again part of a minority group. Now I was

white boy, not Jewboy. It was the same dynamic.

I never fit in. Even in the early days, I was very sensitive and shy. I did not find it easy to dive into group activities like most of the other children. To this day, I can remember standing by the fence, watching the others play ball. I wanted to join them, but I couldn't.

It is not surprising that others felt that I was different and labeled me with whatever racist word was in vogue in the school yard. As a child, my separateness from my brothers and sisters was self-imposed. Others just picked up on my cue and reinforced it. I felt cut off, but I had cut myself off.

I did not feel loved. I did not feel accepted. Being Jewish was just a symbol for feeling lack of love and acceptance in elementary school, just as being white was in junior high school. I chose to be part of a minority group. And I felt all the persecution that generally goes with playing that kind of role.

When Vincent attacked me, I just knew inside that he was perceiving me falsely. So I never felt that I had done anything wrong to deserve the attack. I didn't accept the attack, and so I was not attacked psychologically, even though I had been physically. I stood my ground. He hit me, but I knew that I had done nothing wrong.

Strangely enough, Vincent was a loner too. He felt judged and pushed away by others, and his behavior just reinforced this condition, just as my behavior had reinforced my feelings of separation when I was younger.

It was clear that I had healed a bit by the time I had that encounter with Vincent. I had begun to accept myself. I had begun to reach out to people. I had friends. I had some degree of love and acceptance in my life.

That is what Vincent was attacking. He wasn't attacking me. He was attacking what he thought I had. He was attacking what he thought I had taken away from him.

Perhaps now he knows that there is enough love there for both of us. Perhaps now he has taken responsibility for loving himself and forgiving himself. Perhaps now we can meet as brothers, as equals. I think that is a good possibility. Life has a way of knocking us down or lifting us up depending on which way we threaten the balance.

It is hard for me to come to grips with how I played the victim role growing up, but I must and do see that it was a choice that I made. I felt different from others and I chose to be separate. Vincent felt different from others and he too chose to be separate. We chose different methods for separating ourselves, but the result was the same.

When I feel different from you I attract differences of form. I am Jewish and you are not. I am white and you are not. I am male and you are not. I struggle with these external differences. Sometimes I feel more worthy than you. Sometimes I feel less worthy than you. But I cannot feel equal to you until I accept myself as good, as blameless.

When I know that I am without blame, I can reach out to you. I can never reach out in guilt. Guilt only makes me withdraw or attack.

In the mid-sixties, I became involved in the Committee for Non-violent Action. I lived for a while on the CNVA farm in Connecticut, and later participated on the Boston to Washington March for peace.

I felt committed to the non-violent protest tactics of Gandhi and Martin Luther King. It seemed the only way to end the cycle of violence. One could not pretend that violence did not exist in the world. One had to see the capacity for violence in oneself and in one's brother. However, reacting to violence with more violence was not the answer.

As we walked down Route One through the industrial towns of New Jersey, I felt depressed. The landscape was so ugly. The Vietnam war was ugly too. Did I really think that walking to Washington was going to have an impact on the War? Why was I doing this?

That evening the answer came. We convened a meeting in a local church. We spoke about what was really happening in Vietnam and why we needed to take a stand against it. There were many people there who were sympathetic to our cause, but there was also a fairly large and vociferous group of hecklers. They kept interrupting with comments that questioned our patriotism and integrity.

After the meeting, I heard a voice within me tell me to go up to one of the guys who had been especially negative during the meeting. I approached him. "I'd like to talk to you," I said. He seemed real surprised. It's one thing to make judgments about a group of people, but a little harder to do so with an individual who approaches you in a friendly way.

Here I was the image of everything he detested: a man with a beard and long hair, no doubt a communist and a hippie, afraid to fight for liberty, and probably a drug addict to boot. He probably didn't look much better to me with his crew cut, his hunting jacket, his faced flushed with liquor and self-righteous emotion. Here we were, standing together. I explained who I was and why

I was there. I tried to make myself real to him.

He continued to mouth the same diatribes, but his voice softened a bit with every exchange. In the end, he shook my hand, and said: "I don't agree with you, but I'm glad you came up and talked." At that moment, we were brothers. The war was over. It may not have brought the troops home, but it brought peace to our hearts. Somehow, I felt that this is where the real work of non-violence began, not just in protesting against injustice, but in reaching out to each other as equals, in going beyond our fear and our stereotyped perceptions of each other.

That is the beauty of non-violent action. It offers me a way of standing up for myself without attacking you. Had I been able to do that as a child, I could have become real to my schoolmates and it would have been much harder for them to attack me.

Before I can see my brother's sinlessness, I must see my own. When I am sinless, there is nothing wrong in being Jewish, being white, being sensitive, shy or whatever I am. You cannot attack me when I really accept myself as I am.

You may try to attack me, but I do not accept the attack. It isn't real. Your attack is a cry for love and acceptance. You attack me because you hurt. I see that because I know I am sinless. I know that I do not deserve attack. I know I deserve only love from you.

I do not receive your attack unless I feel guilty, unless I feel I deserve it. My guilt makes your attack real.

As a child, I got what I thought I deserved. Everyone who attacked me gave me what I asked for. I asked for attack and I received it. Others were incidental to the process.

Not accepting myself as I am is an attack against myself. Not accepting you as you are is an attack against you. I cannot attack you unless there is something in you that reminds me of myself. Thus, all attack is self attack.

Being vulnerable means piercing through the defenses I have built against attack. I am hard to love, because I defend against your love. For me, love and hurt go together. I don't want the hurt, so I push away the love.

I don't want to be vulnerable, because I do not want to be hurt. I think that you have the power to hurt me. That is my mistaken belief. That belief causes me to remain hidden in a corner. It causes me to separate myself from you, even as I did as a child.

If you have the power to hurt me, then I better not be with you. I don't want to be hurt. I have been hurt enough.

It is hard for me to face the truth: I am the only one who can hurt me. I am the only one who has hurt me. I don't want to accept that. I don't want to accept responsibility for the fact that I have attacked myself.

Yet until I do so, I cannot heal myself. Only when I know that I am the only one who wounds me will I also understand that I am the only one who can heal me. These two go together.

I am powerful. I have the power to create my life. My power has nothing to do with you. I do not have the power to create your life and you do not have the power to create mine. Each of us is empowered to live the life he has as he would live it.

When I stand up for myself, I witness to my power. I witness to the fact that I make my own choice and you cannot take that choice away from me. Claiming my own power is not attacking you.

It is simply affirming myself.

If I attack you under the guise of affirming myself, then I am trying to be powerful over you. That just betrays my inner sense of inadequacy. I only attack you when I feel there is something lacking in me.

When the *Course* says that attack is not real, it means that it is nonsense. It is a flimsy self-deception. I may try to hold your self deception against you, but if I do I deceive myself. I agree with your mis-perception of me by mis-perceiving you. That is what defending myself is all about.

The *Course* is clear about this. Defense IS attack. When I defend myself, I make myself right and you wrong. I strengthen the wrong by reacting to it. This is where the cycle of violence begins. When Jesus tells us to "resist not evil" he is telling us not to strengthen deception by reacting to it with more deception.

We need to see deception for what it is: mere nonsense. I don't gain anything by confirming your self-deception. The more I confirm it in you, the more you will attack me and others. Rather, I choose to see what you are. You are a sister deceived about who she is. You are trying to control me because you feel out of control. I don't have to be your victim. I don't have to attack you either. I just need to tell you and myself: you are my sister. You are not better or worse than I. You are not less powerful or more powerful. You have the right to decide for yourself, not for me. I support you in deciding for yourself. Please also support me in making my own choice about what's good for me.

We are all equals. We are equally vulnerable. In our acceptance of our vulnerability do we become strong.

I need to reach out to you to discover my strength. I

need to give the love I have to receive yours. I cannot meet my needs for belonging and acceptance by standing in a corner. I must come out and meet you. It is a necessary gesture.

Yet because I reach out to you with love, understanding and support does not mean that I demand that from you in return. I enjoy giving my love to you. It is a fulfillment in itself. As the Course says, "everything I give is given to myself."

My vulnerability is my strength. "In my defenselessness does my safety lie." I claim my humanness and offer to share it with you. There we meet: both looking for love and trying to give it, both hurting and wanting to heal and be whole. In our humanity we meet and discover that God is there with us. Divinity manifests through a human form. Perfection flowers in an imperfect world. Love lives in the lessons I learn and share.

~

THE BUTTERFLY

My humanness is the cocoon in which I nourish and give birth to my divinity. Because I struggle with my ego and all the emotions it evokes does not mean that this struggle describes who I am. But it does describe the process I must go through to realize my freedom.

Dismissing the reality of the cocoon does not help most of us find peace and happiness. It just adds to our confusion and shame. We have a difficult enough time accepting who we are. Denying the reality of our body and the world we live in is just not helpful.   When I feel that my life is barely under control, it is not easy to contemplate having my anchor taken away. Sometimes, it can be dangerous.

So what can I do?

First, it is helpful to accept my physical reality for what it is: a temporary, yet significant learning experience. Then, it is helpful to accept my thoughts and feelings as real. They do have the power to shape my life. And finally, it is helpful to understand that my deepest and truest nature is not limited to the specific thoughts/feelings I have, nor to the body or world I inhabit.

That is to say, I inhabit a vast field of consciousness, only part of which I am aware. As my awareness increases, I discover that I am not who I thought I was.

It is natural for my awareness to increase.   It is the psychological imprint for the physical journey.   I come here to learn, to experience limitation and move beyond it.

I live in this cocoon but my true nature is a butterfly. I do not remember who I am or, if I do, I do not trust myself fully. That is why I cannot toss the cocoon away and rely on my rainbow wings. If I could trust deeply enough, I could do this. Jesus and others have done it. They have healed the sick and raised the dead. They have gone beyond the forms of limitation which are still real to us.

So, I admit, I do not trust myself deeply enough to wriggle out of the cocoon. I need its apparent protection. I need the illusion of time. I need a process whereby I come to trust myself enough to let go .

This is where I am. I know my true nature is the butterfly. It is not something I have to become. It is already there. As I trust in who I am, I begin to emerge from the cocoon.

Emerging is sometimes painful. Growth is sometimes painful. I know that I must give birth to who I am. I know that it is absolutely essential. But I am afraid I might be wrong about who I am. I am afraid it might not work out. I do not trust my sinlessness.

Not trusting my sinlessness is resisting. When I resist I feel pain. When I'm feeling pain, it does not help me to hear you say: "your pain is an illusion. The cocoon is an illusion." What I need to hear is "It's okay. The butterfly is emerging. I can see the tip of its wings. Stay with the pain, for there is an end to it. There is a place where release is found."

Every woman who has given birth to a child knows this process intimately. Few would say that the process was not worth the effort invested in it. Few would say that they did not learn something important about trusting themselves.

We are all in a perpetual state of giving birth to ourselves. And giving birth is all about trust. If I do not trust who I am in the depths of my being, I will hold onto the cocoon. I will hold onto who I think I am.

I am the butterfly, but I believe myself to be the caterpillar. "I am content being a caterpillar," I tell myself. I don't mind crawling. In fact, I prefer it to flying. Why do I have to fly? Why do I have to change? Can't I just stay the way I am right now?"

You see, I have become attached to my image of who I am. I am attached to the form which limits me. I may even recognize that these limits cause my suffering. Yet I may be unwilling to give them up. The pain is familiar.

117

Let me keep what I know, for I am afraid of what I know not.

Being a caterpillar is boring, but safe. Being a butterfly involves some pretty awesome risks. I not sure I'm ready to take them.

The voice of fear can be quite convincing. It is always easier to listen to the voice of fear than it is to listen to the voice of our growth. Fear says: "I hate myself but I hate change more. I must stay in control. I'd rather hate myself and be in control than love myself and be unable to control."

Obviously, the "control" fear wants is illusory. It never really has control over any situation. It just takes the feeling of "wanting control" and places it constantly in our path. That is how it continues to block our growth without delivering to us the safety it promises.

Fear tells me to stop growing. That message is against the imprint of this incarnation. It is against the Tao, the flow of change in which we are all immersed. I simply cannot stop growing, yet I am always trying to do so. That is the victory fear has over me. It never leads me to release, yet it trails behind me, looking over my shoulder, tampering with my life constantly.

Listening to the voice of fear prevents me from entering into the spontaneity of life. It prevents me from being in the heart of the creative process.

Sooner or later, I must level with myself. "No, I am not happy being a caterpillar. I do want to fly, but I am afraid. I want more happiness, but I don't think I deserve it. I want freedom, but I don't feel self-confident enough to trust that I can attain it." In acknowledging my fear and the self-doubt that goes with it, I cease to let it rule me.

Yes, I am afraid, but I am also hopeful, because I see that I am not my fear. My fear is just a voice I hear. I can't pretend that I don't hear it. But I don't need to listen to it either.

I put all my emotional cards out on the table where I can see them and work with them. I come out of the closet. I tell my secrets. I own my fear, so that it will stop owning me.

That is what it means to be honestly in this cocoon. I recognize that the butterfly is what I am, but I also see that I am attached to the caterpillar. I also see that the caterpillar is afraid. It is facing its own extinction.

Any moment of letting go in my life brings up my fear of death. I would like it to be otherwise, but it just isn't. I would like to talk about death confidently, as though I knew exactly what happens when I die and that everything would be okay for me. I would like to do this, but I can't, or I can do it intellectually but I know it is a sham, because I am simply terrified of death.

I am the caterpillar and the caterpillar must die. It does not help me to know that the butterfly will live, if I believe I am the caterpillar. In my attachment to this body, there is fear of extinction. In my attachment to this form, there is resistance to moving to the next. And where there is resistance there is pain.

In my work as a counselor, I am a midwife assisting in the birth process. I see and affirm the butterfly in you, but I also feel your pain and your fear. It is all there together. I know that we can't have one without the other. If there were no caterpillar, there would be no butterfly. Sometimes, we forget that.

THE THERAPEUTIC PROCESS

There is a type of therapy that helps caterpillars cope with being caterpillars. It may be helpful for a while, but it never addresses the spiritual aspirations of the client.

There is also a type of therapy that helps caterpillars pretend that they are butterflies. It may be helpful for addressing small problems, but it never touches the deepest emotional resources of the client, wherein all butterflies are made.

Only an approach that sees both the caterpillar and the butterfly, the pain and the release from pain, can help us move through our growth process consciously, with dignity, opening our hearts as we are ready. It must be a gentle process. It must create a safe space for people to feel the darkness and move through it toward the light.

That kind of therapy empowers. It says to the client "You are the one who knows and you are learning to trust what you know. I do not have the answers for you. I am simply a witness to your process, a fellow traveler who knows something of the process, for it is my process too. I too am awakening to who I am. I too am learning to trust myself."

"I do not stand before you as one who has conquered fear, but as one who has acknowledged it in himself. I do not stand at the end of my journey looking back to you as you undertake yours, but in the middle of it, sharing what I am learning, and learning from what you share with me."

Counselor and client are equals. One does not know more than the other does. It may appear that the therapist knows more than the client. After all, he may have several degrees, many years of experience and be familiar with the latest research. But this means very little to the success of the process.

That is why more informal approaches to the therapeutic process such as co-counseling and twelve step programs are often successful where more formal approaches fail. If you look at the structure of these successful programs and processes, you will see that they assume that healing is a self initiation process in which the helper is essentially equal to one being helped.

It is highly probable that the success of the therapeutic process depends on the mutual acceptance of the following factors:

1. The ability of client and therapist to embrace the goal the client establishes for the therapy and to agree on a tentative time-frame for achieving that goal.

2. The recognition in both client and therapist that the responsibility for achieving that goal rests with the client and that the therapist is simply a witness, helping the client stay focused on the goal, and a facilitator, helping the client recognize and work through the resistance he has in achieving the goal. Both must realize that if there were no inner "resistances" or "blocks" to achieving the goal, the client would have done so already.

3. The commitment both client and therapist make to being honest and fully present with each other in the process. This includes communicating with each other when they feel the process is not working, and revising or re-negotiating the goal and time frame when this

appears helpful to both of them.

4. The understanding that termination is appropriate when the goal has been reached and no new goals have been agreed to by both parties, or when at any time during the process, both parties are unable to agree on "where they are" in the process and "where they are going."

These factors may be simple to understand, but they are difficult to realize. That is because they challenge many of the hidden assumptions behind traditional psychotherapy, such as the concept that the client is sick, does not know what she needs to heal, and is therefore incapable of setting a realistic goal for the therapeutic process.

Our approach is very different. It says point blank that unless the client can set a goal for therapy and take responsibility for it, the process is doomed from the start. To be sure, that goal can be re-negotiated. It is not etched in stone. But it must be established in good faith by the client.

We are saying that unless the therapist can fully embrace the goal and time-frame set by the client, then the therapy will get off on the wrong foot and be a continual push and pull between the needs of the client and the expectations of the therapist. This is anti-therapeutic. It actually does harm rather than help. It would be better for the therapist to opt out of the process than opt into a process she cannot enthusiastically support.

When I go to a travel agent and ask for a ticket to Italy, the travel agent doesn't say: "Why go to Italy? You really belong in China." If he did, I might begin to doubt myself. I might even talk myself into going to China, thinking that the travel agent knows more about such things than I do. In so doing, I do not honor myself.

Of course, the travel agent may be right. Perhaps after going to Italy, I may discover that I really want to go to China. That's fine. Now I can own the journey. If I had to travel to Italy to take responsibility for the trip to China, so be it. I haven't gone backwards at all. I am half-way there. More importantly, now I am ready. Before I was not.

If I went to China before I was ready, I might have come home in alienation and defeat. Going to China when I am ready to go means that I am ready to have my purpose there revealed to me.

It may seem to be a frivolous metaphor, but I really think that a good therapist and a good travel agent have a great deal in common. They both support the client in going where the client feels she needs to go.

It is extremely important for the therapist to recognize that some clients will establish goals that he as a therapist and a person simply cannot support. In this case it is a relief to say "sorry, I can't take you to Italy. Maybe I could try, but I wouldn't feel good about it. Most of my contacts are in the far east. I think it might be better if I refer you to one of my associates who specializes in Mediterranean countries."

Sometimes the client will say: "help me get to Italy" and the therapist will say: "Fine. I have no problem with Italy. I don't sense that that is where you ultimately need to go, but it's on the way. It's a good short term goal. I'd be happy to work with you on it." This kind of negotiation is fine. It is honest and straightforward. Moreover, it may have to be done several times during the process.

"We keep trying to shed our equality, but we cannot do so. It is a condition of who we are. It goes wherever we do."

Over and over again, we must emphasize that clients are responsible for their own healing processes. Many people heal themselves without the aid of a formal helper. That is because healing is a natural, self-initiated process. Sometimes helpers are part of the process. Sometimes they are not.

Unfortunately, we must begin to look at the fact that sometimes helpers actually get in the way of the healing process by encouraging their clients to be dependent on them. This may make the helper feel "important" in the short run, but in the long run it denies the client the only hope for healing that she has. The helper inevitably must wrestle with the disappointment and guilt which arise from taking on a responsibility which was never hers to begin with.

Being a "professional" helper is a dangerous occupation. Here I am trying to help you, and I can barely help myself. If I really buy strongly into my "helper" role, I may make my happiness dependent on my ability to help you. And usually when I do that my ability to help you declines proportionately.

It becomes a "no win" situation. I hate myself because I am unable to help you. The more I hate myself, the more ineffective I become.

My problem, of course, is that I have completely forgotten about you. I have forgotten that your healing is your process, not mine. All I can do is take responsibility for healing myself. And, in this case, that means giving back to you what was never mine for the taking: your responsibility for your healing.

It is ironic. As soon as I step out of my equality with you, I injure myself. I tried to be "the big shot," "the great healer" and ended up feeling miserable.   I went from the mistaken notion that "I can heal you" to the equally mistaken notion that "I can only heal myself by healing you." This is all backwards thinking.

In truth, I cannot heal you, nor can anyone else. You alone can heal yourself. I can offer you a healing relationship perhaps, but only if I am actively taking responsibility for my own healing. If I am not healing myself, I have nothing of significance to share with you.

I am empowered as a "healer" only to the extent that I am healing myself. Then, I am a witness for self-healing. Then, in me, you see the power of your own innocence. That is really where it all begins, in self-acceptance. That is the emotional watershed, where I learn to see myself and others with the eyes of Christ. That is where I embrace the divine vision here and now and take responsibility for manifesting it in my life.

Without my presence, the divine cannot exist here. That does not mean that it does not exist, but it does not exist for me, so it might as well not exist at all. That is why for many years I could not see it. I looked for it everywhere outside of myself. But it was not till I looked within that I found it.

When I see my sinlessness, I also see yours. A therapy that is based on this, is a therapy of love and grace. We deserve no less than this.

~

GOD'S LOVE

My actions show the width and breadth of my heart. Acts of unconditional love, however small, demonstrate that I have welcomed God's messenger into my heart.

Often, I am asked: "How do I hear the voice of Spirit and how do I know that it is really Spirit I am hearing?" The answer is a simple one. The voice of Spirit honors you and others equally. When you listen to the guidance of Spirit, your peace and happiness are restored.

The voice of the ego inevitably reinforces your feeling of separation from your brother or sister. Listening to the voice of the ego — which could be any one of hundreds of old tapes of fear, guilt, hurt, anger, resentment or neglect — disturbs your peace and invites you to attack.

The voice you listen to and obey determines the world you see. The voice of Spirit is a chorus that resonates with equality, purpose and grace, yet it speaks softly. It suggests. It does not demand or play to your guilt. The voice of ego is louder, more demanding. It is always looking to gain an advantage over someone or to protect itself against an advantage it perceives that someone else has.

The voice of ego is provocative. It exaggerates. It makes its point using hyperbole. It blows everything out of proportion. It isolates, condemns, and attacks. It is a brilliant prosecutor. It enlists every raw, unresolved emotion in its cause. It knows how to manipulate the jury to get a conviction.

When we become wise to it, it becomes more subtle. It uses our spiritual concepts to separate us from others. It can be quite sophisticated intellectually. Its arguments are always convincing. It needs to convince us, because deep down inside we feel very uneasy listening to its advice.

Why are we uneasy? Because listening to the ego keeps us chained to the vicious cycle of attack. No matter how much we may buy into "the need for us to attack," none of us enjoys receiving it.

Since all forms of attack are self-attack in disguise, we can only injure ourselves. Thus, every time I attack you, I deepen my own wound. And the more I attack you, the more I postpone my own healing.

Hating ourselves is not a pleasant business. Nevertheless, we are all quite good at it. That is why the true crisis of our time is not the need to love others, but the need to love ourselves.

In truth, except in rare moments, we do not understand what love is. Love cannot flower until attack stops. If we stop attacking, then we make room for love to come through. We remove the block to its presence. Love is not something that comes from us. It comes through us. We just open the channel. We just remove the block.

As long as I take offense, I give offense. Giving offense is attack. As long as I attack you, I attack myself. As long as I attack myself, I cannot feel loved. If I do not feel loved, I will continue to take offense when I perceive that you do not love me. And so the cycle continues.

How then do we remove the blocks to love's presence? We learn to create a psychic space in which we can feel the presence of love. This presupposes that we are preparing for a relationship. Love means nothing without a relationship.

I want to love myself, but I cannot do it. At best, I can accept myself. That clears the space for love to enter.

The whole problem with the "Me Generation" was not selfishness. Selfishness was simply the result of looking for love in material things. It was superficial. It didn't work because it did not lead to self-acceptance.

The "Me generation" is not one generation but many. The development of knowledge has taken an inward turn. We are exploring who we are. We will continue to do so until we understand ourselves at the deepest level.

In exploring, I begin to understand that all of my issues begin with self-acceptance. Accepting myself exactly as I am here and now creates a space in which a "new relationship" begins in my life.

What is this new relationship? It is my relationship with my Source, my universal Father/Mother. It is from this relationship that I feel loved.

I clear this space within me by stopping my attack against myself, and this uncanny love begins to flow through me. As it flows through, I "feel loved." I am not doing the loving. I am receiving it. Someone or something is appreciating me, allowing me to become aware of its presence.

The energy of creation moves in trinity, not in duality. It is not that I cannot talk to God. I can certainly do so. But the means that S/he has given me to speak are through my love for you. By addressing you as one with me, equal with me, so do I bring my Source into direct communion with me.

I would like to make my relationship to my Source a

two-way, private conversation. But my Source resists this desire for privacy on my part. Its love for me is shared with all. As I share it, so do I show my right understanding of, and gratitude for, the love that is freely given to me.

My relationship with God is inseparable from my relationship with you. That is the true meaning of the Trinity. If I feel God's love for me, I will extend it to you. If I don't, I will project my need for love onto you and then, when you don't love me unconditionally, I will attack you.

Our relationship is Holy when we both extend the love we feel in our hearts to each other. That love does not come from us. It comes through us. And so it can never be possessive or manipulative in any way.

When I extend God's love to you, it is not something that I am "doing." I am merely reflecting to you the love that I receive in its entirety without judgment or precondition of any kind. In the same way, when the moon is full, it reflects the totality of the sun's light to earth.

You, my brother and sister, are like the full moon shining the light of the Source to me. When you are filled with the Holy Spirit, you remind me of who I really am. You show me the light of creation in all its glory. What would I do without your witness? What would you do without mine?

In the darkness of self-deception I walk. The sky is heavy with clouds. I have forgotten about light. I doubt that it ever existed. And then, I see a shimmer at the billowy edge of darkness. The clouds open to your face. You have hidden in the darkness to comfort me. I see the soft glow of moonlight on your skin, yet I hardly recognize you in your fullness. Indeed, it seems as if the face of Christ himself has come to shine on me.

And all this because we are here together. Who would sacrifice this blessing for some lonely, private salvation, even if it were possible? No I cannot look upon you now without extending my hand to you.

You have witnessed to what is deepest in my heart. You have gathered the stale weeds into flame. You have kindled the forlorn light, the forgotten promise. You have taken my hand and led me forth. How can I refuse to do the same for you, my brother?

If one sister has shown me the light, then all have shown me. Let me not judge the one who cowers before me and looks away when I look at her, for this is the very one who reached out to me in my need. This is the one who remembered me. She feels forgotten now, and so God has brought me to her side. I do not try to love her, for I know nothing of love, but I extend to her the divine love I feel in my heart.

The divine messenger does not know how to love but trusts that the universal Father/Mother does. Thus do we each bring the face of Christ to each other.

THE ATONEMENT
IS A RELATIONSHIP PROCESS

My world is peopled by my perceptions. All of my perceptions are for or against. That is the nature of perception. That is the nature of the world.

I create what I desire. I also create what I fear. I also desire what I fear and fear what I desire. Herein lie the self-imposed conflicts of my life. Herein lie the lessons I have come to learn.

If I desire you or fear you I cannot see you. I see what my desire wants to see, or what my fear wants to see. This has nothing to do with who you are. It has nothing to do with who I am. It has only to do with my desire or my fear.

My desires consume everything, yet still I am not satisfied. My fears cause me to run from everything, yet still I do not feel safe. My hardest lessons are my simplest ones: My desires cannot satisfy and my fears cannot keep me safe.

Desire and fear together make the net of perception. Everything in this net is illusory. It is a whole bundle of illusion. It cannot be dismantled piece by piece. The whole bundle must be discarded.

If I want to see you as you are I cannot have preconceptions or expectations of you. I must meet you in the present, without words or concepts. If I bring the past, I will see the past. If I bring the future, I will see the future. You do not exist in either the past or the future. If there is a you that exists in the past or the future it is part of that bundle of illusory images I need to discard.

Meeting you means joining with you. Not meeting you means forcing us together or apart. Whatever can be forced together or apart is not you or me but part of that bundle of illusions.

You and I can only meet. Meeting does not mean merging, nor does it mean having rigid boundaries. It means being together with our boundaries touching. It means crossing back and forth over those boundaries, as people in border towns continuously cross back and forth. I move in spaces that you call your own and vice versa. When we feel attacked by each other, we struggle to uphold our boundaries. When we feel needy, we can't wait to tear them down.

The act of meeting occurs when I feel at ease with you, when I am neither moving toward you nor moving away, when I am simply enjoying your presence next to me. That is the moment of balance, of equality, of complementarity, of complete resonance. That is the moment when Christ stands with us. His being is engendered by our equal relationship. That is why Jesus says: "whenever two or more come together, I will be with them."

In our meeting, I experience my perfection and you experience yours. That perfection does not exist outside our relationship, only within it, for life IS relationship.

As soon as I see anything other than equality in our relationship, our relatedness begins to wither and I lose sight of my perfection and yours. At that moment, we move apart. In that moment I lose my sinlessness and you lose yours. That moment is "the fall from grace."

We always "fall" together. Two, not one, were expelled from the Garden of Eden. The expulsion of Adam and Eve must therefore be seen not only as a reflection of their relationship with God, but as a reflection of their relationship with each other. Indeed, when God asked Adam why he ate of the forbidden fruit, he refused to take responsibility. "The woman gave me and I did eat," he replied. Is this not the first instance we see of projection?

Adam blamed Eve and Eve blamed the serpent. Yet, in truth, each was responsible only for the choice he or she made. Taking responsibility would have kept them in or close to the garden. There, they would have had to continue to wrestle with the serpent (the dark side) to integrate it, but they would not have internalized it as shame.

Having lived for so long with the sword of darkness held above our heads, we too must retrace our steps back to the garden. We must surrender the sword of shame and return to the task of wrestling with the serpent. We must take responsibility for our own darkness and stop projecting it onto each other. That is the way back to God.

The tragedy of Adam and Eve is the degradation of their relationship from a free and abundant one to a co-dependent one. As we know, their offspring — Cain and Able — did not do much better. This tragedy is as alive today in our relationships as it was then.

So let us remember that all life IS relationship. We do not fall from grace alone, but together, nor can we return alone, but only side by side. My awareness of your sinlessness and my own brings me back into a state of grace. Nothing else will do this.

The "atonement" is simply our process of coming back together again, just as "the fall" was our process of coming apart. The statement "I Re-cognize All Being One" — the umbrella title for these writings — is the clarion call of the atonement. Wherever we go, we go together. Together we have fallen, and together we will rise again.

The story of "the fall" and "the return" is a myth. It is not history. History is something that took place in one time. It belongs to the past. Myth is something that takes place in all times. It is an eternal thread, as true now as it was then. Neither the "fall from grace" nor the "atonement" belong to history. They belong to myth. They are not stories about a particular time, but about all times, and about the nature of time itself.

Right now in our relationships, we choose to meet or to separate. Our relationships are the ground on which the myth is played out. This is the Holy Instant, the moment of choice. We have been here before and we will be here again, until we make the choice that honors all of us.

~

CREATION

Only when I enter the garden of my innocence, can I create. Until then, my "creations" are merely reflections of my own desire or fear.

Until I experience my sinlessness, I cannot witness to the abundance of creation. For abundance does not come from desire, nor does it come from fear.

Both desire and fear are conditions of scarcity. When I desire, I want what I do not have. When I fear, I am afraid that what I have can be taken away.

The abundant heart of all creation knows nothing whatever of scarcity. Scarcity is an erroneous belief imposed on the spontaneous flow of Tao, which is Mother of us all. The great Mother does not withhold from her children.

Her children do not always get what they want when they want it, and they may respond by crying, sulking, or throwing temper tantrums. It doesn't matter. It doesn't do any harm, nor does it do any good. "No praise; no blame," as the I Ching would say. You can't push the river, nor can you hold it back, no matter how hard you try.

The river of life brings its abundance to all of us as we are ready to embrace it. If I feel worthy, that which I value will flow to me. If I feel unworthy, I will not receive what I value for what I value reinforces my unworthiness. But I will receive what I need.

I may not accept that gift, because I prefer another

one, but that is my choice. Making that choice means staying in illusion. It means turning away from my abundance.

Nevertheless, the gift is not withdrawn just because I have chosen not to receive it. Mother may ignore my fears or my desires, but She never refuses to meet my needs. That is Her great beauty. She continues to offer Her simple gift to me, no matter how much I complain, no matter how many temper tantrums I have. Her gift is always there for me. I need choose only to receive it.

When I impose my belief in scarcity on the world, I place conditions on my happiness. I say: "I can only be happy if I get a well paying job, if I find a loving relationship, if I get out of debt, or if I get my book published," an so on. I make my happiness conditional upon something else.

If my happiness is dependent on certain results, then I am doomed to unhappiness. Whenever I want something so much that I make my happiness conditional upon receiving it, that is a sure sign that I am afraid to receive it. Think about it for a moment. If I were not afraid of it, it would be easy for me to receive it.

My intense desire for something or someone merely masks an internal feeling of inadequacy which I inappropriately seek to have filled from the outside. My inadequacy actual fuels my desire and that intensity scares others away. They can sense my desperateness. They feel manipulated and they withdraw.

I scare away what I seek. If I do this, I must conclude that either I don't really want it or I am afraid to receive it. Actually both are true.

This issue of scarcity vs. supply exists at many different

levels. We must be careful not to be confused by the levels on which it operates.

As a son or daughter of God, what I want and what I need are one and the same. Whatever I want with my whole being will come to pass, because I need it for my growth. And what is given to me for my growth is given, not just to me, but to all humankind.

Do I create what I want? Yes, at a deep level of understanding, I always create what I want. I may not consciously know that this is what I want — in fact, I may be convinced that it is NOT what I want — but since it is what I need it is also what I want.

I cannot grow if I do not cooperate with what I need. My needs cannot be ignored or dismissed. Ignoring my needs for security and belongingness will not help me become a spiritual person. It will just create a deeper schism between what I need and what I want.

Connecting my needs and my wants is an essential task of true spiritual work. Conscious and unconscious must be joined together. Male and female must be brought together. Thoughts and feelings must be gathered together. Spiritual work is the work of wholeness, of integration. It is the process by which I learn to accept all of myself, all of you, all of my life.

I must remember that, at the deepest level, whatever is happening in my life is happening with my permission! If I give that permission consciously, then I am creating what I want, because I am in touch with my deepest needs. If I give that permission unconsciously, then I am not creating what I want, because I am not in touch with my deepest needs.

Consciously creating what I want requires the

integration of my feelings and my thoughts. Often, what I "think" I want is not what I want with my whole being. Deep down, I have feelings which want something very different. These feelings are in touch with my deepest needs, many of which are so exaggerated and contorted they could not possibly be met.

Listening to my feelings is reaching out to the inner child. It is not necessary that the child get exactly what she demands, but she must be given a fair and loving hearing. Bringing the child and adult together is same process as bringing thoughts and feelings together.

When thoughts and feelings are brought together, they give birth to intuition. Intuition invites the dance of reason and emotion. It invites a synthesis. And this synthesis in turn brings what I want into harmony with what I need.

Then, and then alone, can I consciously create my life. Then, my dialogue is no longer with myself and my projections, but with my brother and sister, for together our challenge is to create a world that meets all of our needs.

Our founding fathers gave us a great road map. They understood that life, liberty, and the pursuit of happiness must be the inheritance of all. Yet many who follow in their footsteps have lost the way. They have approached the journey without inner direction. Until they find that direction, they are like the blind leading the blind.

I cannot make peace with my brother until I have ended the war within myself. It is my war, not my brother's. If I bring it to him, he will think it real and join with me or against me in the fight. I will have done both of us a disservice.

Let me understand that my only battle is with myself.

Once I have won that battle, I can resolve any conflict. I can solve the most complex problems. For I become a co-Creator with the universal mind.

What I create is what I need. What you create is what you need. Our needs are not competitive, but complementary. When complementary needs are met, great energy is produced. With that energy behind us, even difficult things can be accomplished. We move with the flow, not against it. Miracles occur naturally.

True creation is not a "doing," but a "letting be done." That is why we call it co-creation. The intelligence behind creation does not come from us, but moves through us. We allow love to pass through us. We are its channel. We allow light to pass through us. We are its lens.

Our work is not the work of "doing," but the work of alignment. As we become aligned within, we become a useful channel for the Creator's work. Then S/he can work through us. Then our purpose can become clear to us.

Whatever that purpose is, we can be sure that it benefits others as much as it benefits us. It is a gift of love to all who receive it. What else could God give to me or through me but such a gift?

When I say "Thy will be done," I am acknowledging the presence of a universal intelligence in my life. I know that only that intelligence can anticipate and meet my deepest needs and those of my brother and sister. I invite that intelligence to work through me to meet all needs that arise, including my own. I trust in this and witness to its healing power. For apart from It, I am but an empty shell, yet joined with It, I am the very instrument of Creation.

SPECIAL RELATIONSHIPS

I cannot surrender to God until I accept my equality with all beings. When I violate that essential equality in my thoughts and in my actions, I cease to be a channel for infinite love.

My relationship with Spirit is infinite and unbounded. It is a surrender to that completeness in myself which I sense but cannot explain or define. My body/mind is just a vehicle in which this completeness can express itself. My life is just a channel in which Spirit lives, and breathes, and has Its Being.

My body/mind and my life belong either to me or they belong to the Infinite Intelligence. If they belong to me, then I shall only have them for a time. If they belong to Infinite Intelligence, then I never really had them, at least not exclusively.

I cannot lose what I never had. I can only lose what I have or appear to have.

What, then, do I have but an illusion of authorship over myself, my life, and over you and yours? My need to manipulate you or be possessive of you is simply a projection of my need to possess myself. Possessing myself means kicking God out. It means claiming authorship and denying that my authority comes from God.

All possession is object relationship or, as Martin Buber would say, it belongs to the world of "I-It." The "I" of "I-It" is an illusory "I," just as the "It" of "I-It" is an illusory "It."

When I see you as a body, as a belief, a package of thoughts and feelings, a form of any kind, I have resigned both you and myself to the world of illusion. This "I" that sees you as "It" is ego.

By contrast, when I see you as Spirit, as unlimited and whole, I have entered the world of "I-Thou." I have taken a stand in my equality with you. In that equality, Spirit remains.

The thought of "I-It" gives birth to the illusory world of "I-It." Everything that happens in that world is an attempt of a Subject to remake itself into an Object through projection. This is the world of special relationships, for in this world, every relationship I have is threatened by every other relationship. In this world, relationships are commodities competing for my attention. I become invested in them in the same way that I become attached to material possessions. They are, indeed, just different forms of the same attachment.

I can only withdraw from that world by seeing myself and you differently. Only when I see you and myself as equal do I see either one of us correctly, and so only then can I meet you in genuine relationship. That is the "I-Thou" experience. That is a holy relationship.

When I address you as Thou, as brother or sister, I am already related to you. It matters not what I say, for whatever I say to a brother or sister must be said in truth.

When I address you as It, as an object of my desire or fear, I have cut off my relationship not only with you, but with myself. It doesn't matter what I say, for everything I say merely demonstrates my pain and my feelings of alienation from you and from myself.

When the primary word "I-Thou" is spoken, God is

present therein, and therefore so am I. When the primary word "I-It" is spoken, God cannot enter, and so neither can I. I have created a world which I cannot enter. I am held hostage by my own thought system.

All of us take a stand in relationship or outside of it. He whom I perceive as different from myself offers me the opportunity to accept my equality. If I accept him I say "Thou," and God speaks with me. If I judge or reject him, then I say "It" to both of us and, where "It" is, God cannot be.

Every time I address my sister, I also address God. The importance of this cannot be overemphasized.

It is a mistake to think that some of our relationships are holy relationships and others are special relationships. All of our relationships are holy relationships. We either recognize them as such or we don't.

I am given the opportunity to say Thou or It in every moment. It matters not that I have said Thou or It to you before. Because I have said Thou before does not mean that I cannot mis-perceive you now. And because I have said It before does not mean that I cannot for the first time see you as you really are.

Relationships are seen truly or devalued in each moment. Every time I say "It" I keep myself an object and victim of the world. Every time I say "Thou" I awaken to who I am and begin to cross the Bridge.

~~~

THE MYTH OF ROMANTIC LOVE

We all want to be loved and accepted as we are. Yet for most of us this a rare experience.

As we grew up, our parents and significant others primarily demonstrated conditional love to us. Every experience of conditional love fed our ego's development and our perception of the world around us as a dangerous place to be. We learned well to attack and defend. We never learned to choose love. And we never experienced the world that could be created out of our choice for love.

For most of us, only when our pain and suffering became unbearable, only when we were brought to our knees, did we consider choosing love instead of fear. Yet that consideration was the foundation of a new experience of life.

Choosing to love you in difficult situations, is a choice that lifts me up. It makes "me" feel better. I may think I am loving "you" but, in fact, I am loving myself too.

Loving you is a gift I give to myself. Loving you helps me bring love to the part of me that feels wounded, the part of me that is in need of love. Accepting and loving you just as you are brings a wave of warmth into my being. I feel my own wholeness in my acceptance of yours.

Such love is always unconditional. It ever says Thou. It blesses me fully, because it is given to you without strings attached. Whatever I give to you I give to myself.

"When we see from truth
we take total responsibility
for every situation in our
lives. There are no exceptions. Every situation, every
relationship, every event
reflects the consciousness
that created it."

When I look to you to meet my needs, I address you as "It." In looking to get, I forget to give, and so withhold the gift from myself.

When I fall in love with you, I enter the world of Thou with you. We seem to anticipate each other's needs. My deepest desire is to please you and to comfort you and vice versa. We are blissful. We experience life as timeless. Each moment is an eternity.

But then something happens. We start to expect a certain attention and responsiveness from each other, and we are hurt and resentful when our expectations are not met. We begin to erect defenses to protect ourselves from disappointment. We lose our vulnerability, our willingness to trust each other implicitly. And everything that love made between us, now fear begins to tear down.

That is the typical upward and downward trajectory of most romantic relationships. They raise our expectations and then deflate them suddenly. Such experiences are often catastrophic in our lives. We just don't understand what went wrong. We begin to question our worthiness to love and be loved at the deepest level.

It is not that our experience of "Thou" is unreal, so much as it is that we are unable to sustain it. Gradually the world claims our attention and we find it more and more difficult to give it to each other. "I-Thou" disintegrates into "I-It."

When the world intrudes into our relationships, we either lift it up into the sanctity of our loving embrace, or we allow it to drag us down. In the former case, our holy relationship is extended to others. In the latter, we seek to keep the relationship exclusively for ourselves, and so make it competitive and worldly.

Love comes into our relationships through our ability to love and accept each other unconditionally. As soon as our love becomes conditional, the channel is closed and love is obscured.

Our ability to love and accept one person unconditionally is testimony to our ability to love and accept all. What I give to one sister, I give to all. Unconditional love is not exclusive. It is all inclusive. All are welcomed here.

That is why this relationship is holy. Let one brother or sister be rejected here, and our relationship contracts in fear.

To restore its holiness requires a change in our perception of what our relationship is for. We are together not just for our mutual satisfaction, but for our mutual growth. Together we receive more than we could receive separately, and our combined energies reach to places we cannot anticipate. The more who are welcomed within, the wider the channel grows and the further it reaches. That is the process of God's extension.

Resisting that extension can be a painful affair since it tends to restrict our mutual growth in the relationship. And if we are not growing together, then we start growing apart.

The myth of romance is deceptive, not because it suggests that two beings can join together, but because it suggests that they can do so exclusively. That is the ultimate conceit. For in every meeting of two beings, another one is present. In the world of "Thou," you and I meet in God. And His agenda may be different from our own.

THE UNFOLDING OF PURPOSE

Understanding ourselves and understanding God's plan for us are one process, not two. Purpose comes from self-acceptance. It comes from expressing our unique talents and abilities in every way that life offers us.

Each of us must "come out" of hiding. Our special talents are not meant just for us but for our family, our friends, and our communities. Each of us has been given a gift to be shared with others. Trusting that gift enough to share it is the first step in self-actualization.

Aiming too high can be a big problem. If I think that my gift is significant only if I can share it with thousands of people, then I will neglect the opportunity I have to share it with a couple of my friends. When I set up criteria for giving my gift and expectations for how it will be received, I tamper with my own creative process.

Giving what I have is empowering. It creates energy and enthusiasm in my life. I need that energy and enthusiasm to extend my gift to all who may benefit from it. It does not matter who or how many they are. It is not up to me to place limits of any kind upon the gift, for the gift does not belong to me, but rather to those who needs it addresses.

When I began teaching, I used to be disappointed if only a few students showed up. I took that as a criticism of me. Then, it became clear to me that having a few students in class was an opportunity to work at a more profound level. The small classes provided students with an intimate atmosphere where participation was easy for them. In a larger group, they might not have felt as comfortable sharing.

There might have been a time in my life when I would have turned away from this opportunity to share because it did not meet my expectations. In so doing, I would have blocked my self expression and judged not only the situation, but myself, as wanting.

I cannot learn to trust my gift if I do not give it. If I am not giving it, it is not because of "poor luck" or because life is not cooperating with me, but because I am afraid to trust it. I am afraid perhaps that others will not appreciate me, or that I will not live up to my own expectations. Or perhaps I am afraid that I don't really have a gift to give. In my fear, I create constant barriers to sharing my gift. And so I never share it.

In order to break the cycle of self-denial, I must consciously accept one of the many "low threat" opportunities which life offers to me for sharing. The next time I find myself judging the invitation to participate because it does not meet my expectations, let me pause and say: "Yes, I would be happy to come."

Often we use money or prestige as an excuse for why we do not share our gift. "I won't do that workshop because it will not pay enough" or "I can't do that on a volunteer basis, because it won't pay the bills." By taking such an attitude, I am putting something between my need to express myself and the fulfillment of that need. That "something" just happens to be money.

I don't feel valued unless I'm paid or otherwise appreciated in concrete ways. I feel that I'm giving something away for nothing. I believe the gift is "mine" and that I can choose not to give it.

This is not true. The gift isn't mine. It has been given to me in trust. That trust assumes my need to pass the gift on as an essential ingredient in my process of self-actualization. If I do not give the gift, I cannot experience it. Experiencing the gift and giving it are the same process.

Holding onto my gift is an attempt to experience it without giving it. It is an attempt that invariably fails. For that failure I blame you ("you prevented me from giving my gift"), or I blame myself ("I just don't have the self-confidence or the ability to give this gift"), or I blame God ("I don't really have a gift to give; the idea that I have a gift is just wishful thinking"). Often, I run all these tapes at the same time.

My problem begins with the issue of authorship. I am not the gift, but the giver of that gift. As the giver, all I can do is recognize when life provides me with an opportunity to pass the gift on. In the act of passing it on, I experience the gift. Only in passing the gift on do I experience its meaning, its true value.

When I make money more important than giving the gift, I am making a clear statement: "Making money is more important than my self-actualization." It suggests that some external reward system determines the value of what I have to give and, by reference, my value as well.

How can some external system of weights and measures evaluate God's gift to me or my success in giving it? If it could, all people in touch with their God-nature would be rich and all others would be poor. Clearly this is not the case, nor is the opposite true. Poverty may

" Loving you is a gift I give to myself. I feel my own wholeness in my acceptance of yours."

help some people be aware of what's most important in life, but poverty in and of itself does not being people closer to God.

Our external systems of rewards simply cannot evaluate the gift that lies in each of our heart's. Nor, for that matter, can we evaluate it. We know not what the gift is for until we begin to give it.

Then, our purpose unfolds. Then, doors are opened. Often they are different doors than the ones we expected to be open to us. That's okay. It does not matter that we did not understand the whole direction when we began to take the first few steps. We simply knew that those steps were appropriate ones. We were ready to take them. We were ready to trust. Indeed, we never really know more than that. That understanding in the Holy Instant is sufficient.

Looking back at whence we have come, we can see the continuity of our journey. Surely, there have been tiresome detours, wrong turns, and cul-de-sacs for all of us. But each of us has also occasionally found our direction, for each of us has at times trusted the gift and allowed our giving of it to guide us. Those times represent key markings in our lives. They show us where we have come from and where we are going.

We do not need a more specific course. A more detailed road map would be misleading, for one wrong turn might make the entire map obsolete. God prescribes less and forgives more. Each choice places us at the beginning.

We can always get where we are going from here. It might mean backtracking, but the way is there. If it weren't, then the gift would be unreal, for the direction would be meaningless.

So here I am and it is okay. It is a good starting point. I don't really know where I'm going, and that's okay too. The gift is buried deep inside of me. I do not feel its presence, so it's hard for me to trust it. It's hard for me to believe that I have a purpose.

It's okay. This is where I begin. Attempting to begin anywhere else would be dishonest.

My task in the present is to feel the presence of the gift, not as something that I own, but as something that has been entrusted to me. My task is to see that whenever I have taken up that trust and expressed this gift, I have felt joy and wonder. I have felt the presence of truth within as a deep abiding integrity and others have felt it too.

Let me find only two instances of self acknowledgment and expression and I have found enough direction to begin. I know now what the next step is. And that is all I need to know.

My work is not to find out more, but to practice what I know. That means that I accept the next opportunity life offers me to express the gift, regardless of the terms that are offered. I have made an inner commitment and that commitment needs to be fulfilled.

If I find fault with the form, I will not use it. I will place still another block between myself and my fulfillment. Let me not focus on the specific form, but see the opportunity it provides me. The form itself is not important. It is its function which is important.

When I accept the opportunity that comes to me, I begin to get in touch with my own function, my own purpose. Now there is movement in my life. Now there is direction. Now there is energy and interest. Now there is positive expectation.

I don't know what will happen but I know that it will be okay. I know that I will be able to embrace the situation, whatever it is.

If I am waiting for someone else to show me the way, then I am waiting in vain, for the way opens from within. Nobody else can plot my course. Even I cannot plot my course without listening deeply.

If I am expecting others to support me in my choice, then I am undermining the power of that choice by projecting some part of my responsibility for it. Help and support may come and I can accept them with gratitude, provided that they are offered voluntarily and without strings attached.

My purpose is related to yours, yet I cannot find it as long as I insist that your purpose be the same as mine. Each of us needs to honor what is deepest in us. I must not make demands upon my brother which take him from his purpose, nor should I allow him to make such demands upon me. My ability to be true to myself does not hinder my brother. It helps him.

If I can help my sister fulfill her purpose, then I should do so. The time and energy I offer her is not taken away from my own purpose, but added to it. For every time I help my sister awaken to her purpose, I fulfill another aspect of God's plan.

As I learn to give without expectation of return, my relationship to supply begins to change, and so does my relationship with my brother. We are not competing for goods which are limited and in short supply, but generating goods and services which are limited only by the need for them.

If we support each other fully in doing what we do

well and with joy, we will meet that need without struggling. But if we seek to hold each other back, for fear that the success of one undermines the success of the other, then neither of us fulfill our purpose and those who need our gifts will not have them.

It is a simple proposition, but one that goes against everything that we have come to believe. My purpose is not at odds with yours, but joined in ways I will only come to know by following it and encouraging you to follow yours. We are not competitive but complementary in our needs and our ability to meet them.

If I do not trust the gift within me enough to give it when and where it is needed, without being concerned with guarantees of recompense, I can never know the fruits of the divine economy. Instead, I will succumb to the economy of fear and put my shoulder behind the wheel of manipulation and pain. That is the choice I made yesterday, and the choice I face again today.

I must begin where I am. And, as the Talmud says: "if not now, when?"

~~

REALITY AND ILLUSION

It seems simplistic, yet we must say it over and over again until it finally sinks in: Reality is self acceptance and everything that flows from it. From my self acceptance comes:

1. my awareness and integration of my shadow & my ability to heal the wounded child within;
2. my ability to take responsibility for my life and withdraw the projection of my weaknesses and strengths onto you;
3. my ability to accept you as you are here and now, even when you don't meet my demands or expectations;
4. my awareness of my purpose as a gift that needs to be shared with you and others in my life;
5. my ability to let go of my need to control my life and increasing openness to the opportunities life provides me for my awakening;
6. my ability to support you in your journey and to accept your support for mine.

In short, from my self acceptance flows the actualization of my abilities in the world through joining with you and others in mutually supportive relationships. Happiness and peace are the results of my process of coming to embrace myself.

By contrast, Illusion is self-condemnation and

everything that is built upon it. From my inability to accept myself comes my condemnation of you and my feeling that I must compete with you for love and for supply. My sense of inadequacy is projected onto every situation in my life, resulting in conflict in my thoughts and in my relationships.

The illusory world that arises from self judgment has its own laws. They are the laws of projection, whereby manipulation and attack are justified and confirmed. This is the world that we call "real," because it seems to exist outside of us. Yet insight tells us that this outer world begins within. If it is "real," it is real only because we believe it to be so.

When we question the single false belief about ourselves upon which this world is built, we begin to see that its "reality" is flimsy indeed. Take away my judgment of myself and the whole world of pain and suffering begins to slip away. It was but a shadow anyway, built upon other shadows. It was my belief that made those shadows seem real. Without the meaning I gave them, they had no real stature. Without the breath I breathed into them, they could not move.

I am the architect of my own pain with all its contorted shapes pretending to be real. And I am the one who awakens and walks free from the world I made to another one made not by me. I am the one who awakens to my innocence, my goodness, my implicit acceptability.

LETTER TO MY SISTER

This morning I arise before dawn, bearing dreams. I need to see this day begin. I need to feel the heart-red light of forgiveness to meet you in a way that dignifies us both. I need to speak to you as to a child I love, my own child and yours. For both are hurt and both need the healing rays of dawn to strengthen them for today's journey.

Last night when you hung up the phone in anger, I felt: "Good. I'm glad you want to leave. The relationship is not affirming to me. I no longer want to be a target for your criticism."

Those last few words are so important. They are true. I don't want to be a target for your anger and judgment. But the conclusion is false. I don't want you to leave. I love you. You are my sister. I have learned much from you. I want to continue to learn from you, and I want you to see how you can learn from me.

I am glad you experienced some anger. That anger is the door to truth. It seems to be anger at me, but it is really aimed at yourself. You don't like yourself when you judge me. You don't like yourself when you have expectations of me which I don't meet, no matter how justified you think they are. You don't like yourself when you are unable to find the compassion and the tolerance in your heart to love and accept me as I am.

So why should I take offense at your anger? It is not meant for me, though you would place it at my feet. Yet

158

I can learn from it too. I see how I disappoint you. You are upset when I am late and remind me over and over again. You are upset when I miss a meeting, because you feel that I am not there for you. You feel that you are offering more than you are receiving in return. You wish to replace me, to find someone else who can give to you as you would have him give. I see that all your desire for companionship with another being, and with a man in particular, comes into this. I feel your deep disappointment, your despair. I see how you alienate those who love you best. I see how you attack them and push them away.

But I will not go away so easily, sister. I love you. There is something of truth in everything that you have ever said to me. I have always listened for that, even when your insight came to me in the shape of an expectation or demand I could not meet.

For my part, I do not want you to make demands on me or judgments about me. They do not help you or me. They merely show me that I am inadequate in your eyes.

I don't accept that idea. It isn't true. I know I am not the contorted picture you present to me. So I do not feel wounded, yet a little hurt remains. And that little hurt is still an offense I have taken, for I see myself rising to my own defense. And I do not need to defend myself, for there is nothing lacking in me.

We are both beings who have temporarily forgotten that we are completely sufficient and acceptable as we are. You do not need what you demand from me, nor do I need to withhold it from you.

I want to use this moment of daybreak, at the edge of hurt and anger, to explore the truth. For there is something here, deep down for me. Everything that happens in my life brings a lesson for me. Your anger and my hurt bring a lesson for both of us.

I can feel you push me away, and I like it. Does this seem strange? I can't wait to end this relationship because it seems to be such a thorn in my side. It takes all my commitment to hang in there. That's ironic, because that is what you asked for from me, is it not? Beneath your unreal judgment of me was a simple request for commitment, for a demonstration of my love for you.

And now you have it, not perhaps as you requested it, but my commitment rises to meet you now. It rises toward you, even though my ego would have me run away and never see you again.

I can see how the little hurt I nurse opens a deep wound. Entering that wound is like returning to my childhood. In that wound is all the pain I feel, all the pain I have ever felt. In that wound is all the judgments about myself which I have internalized. In that wound is the belief that I am not okay, that something is wrong with me, because I am unable to be what others expect me to be.

I could not meet my mother's expectations. I was not the polite, cheerful, cooperative child she requested. I did not perform very well the unwritten script she gave to me at birth. So there was often disappointment in her eyes when she looked at me. Not that she did not love me. In fact, in some ways she loved me too much. Her love was controlling. It demanded from me something I could not give.

Growing up I learned two ways of dealing with my mother's emotional demands: emotional withdrawal and rage. I learned both from my father. When my mother approached me with heavy demands, I hid in an emotional corner. I withdrew part of myself and buried it deeply. I felt I had to bury it to retain it. My father did much the same thing. Of course, when we withdrew emotionally from her, my mother felt dishonored and she demanded even more. Finally, when I was trapped by her relentless pursuit, I lashed back at her in rage. As an adolescent, I was able to express a great deal of that pent up anger. My father, however, was able to express very little of his rage. Instead, he withdrew permanently. He asked my mother for a divorce. Again, she felt abandoned.

Only now, after being divorced for 25 years, are my mother and father ready to heal some of their old wounds. It is a beautiful thing to see them approaching each other again, with caring and respect. I guess that is what this journey is all about. We are here to heal. Yet we cannot heal until we are ready.

So, my sister, I ask you to realize that when you make demands of me, I want to run a hundred miles an hour away from you. I want to lose myself in some mountain cave on the other side of the earth. Like an animal burrowing in for winter's sleep, I want to become inaccessible. I don't want you to find me. I would rather that you left me alone.

But, you know, that's only the voice of fear in me speaking. That is just the defense mechanism of a child who has been emotionally violated and does not want to be hurt again. Really, this child does not want you to leave. He wants you to stay and love him.

That, of course, must be your choice. You may choose

love or fear in this situation. My choice cannot be dependent on yours.

I must choose to love this child, because he is part of me. I am not always proud of him. Sometimes I look at him in the same way my mother did. After all, I have internalized those old judgments. They are my way of continuing to beat myself. I do not need my mother for that anymore. I am eminently capable of doing it all by myself.

When my sister judges me, it reinforces my self-judgment. Yet I am learning to recognize that internal voice as the voice of fear. I am learning to respond to that voice lovingly without giving in to its desire to withdraw from conflict situations in my life. I am learning to say: "It's okay that you are afraid. It's perfectly natural under the circumstances. You are judging yourself unworthy and withdrawing is your way of protecting yourself. Look deeply now. Another is not attacking you. That is just what seems to be happening. Another is just holding up a mirror for you. At the deepest level, you must choose whether to see the mirror as a weapon or as an opportunity to see the truth about yourself. Seeing that truth is never easy. It is never easy to acknowledge that you attack yourself."

So, my friend, I see that you have once again provided me with an opportunity to look at myself and I thank you for that. I hope this situation works in the same way for you.

I am changing deeply in my life. I see how I have become my mother, making emotional demands on others that they cannot possibly meet. I have done that, and so when you do it, it is not hard to recognize. You see, sister, forgiving your attack is really just forgiving myself for my own attack against others and ultimately against myself.

I also see how I have become my father, withdrawing from situations which make emotional demands upon me. So when you withdraw from me, it is a familiar move. I like it. It seems to give me permission to do the same. But doing that is not good for me. Doing that is an admission that I am unworthy of love. And this is not the case. For truly, I am worthy of your love. I am not the one who disappoints you. I am not the guilty one you see, but your sinless brother.

Please understand that I will never be able to meet your expectations, nor will you be able to meet mine. We both struggle with the pain of this all the time. We look to others to fulfill our needs and, when they don't, we become demanding. That only deepens our separation. Others always run from our demands or oppose them with their own. There is no peace in this.

Demanding love gives no peace to either of us.

So it seems there is nowhere else to go from here, but to reach out to each other with open arms. That, I guess, is what this letter attempts to do. May it not be found wanting in that respect. May the light of dawn shine through this and be felt affirming the rising sun in you. For you are my sister, the only sister I have. You are not dispensable. You cannot be replaced. Without you, I cannot realize own my divinity, for there is nothing in you which is not also in me.

Your ego reflects my own. Your hurt is in my heart as deeply as my own, for it is one hurt. We all feel it. The trigger may be different for each of us, but the pain is the same.   And that pain is a door that opens to self-acceptance and compassion for one another, if we allow it.

Shall we hold the hurt? If so, we acknowledge the attack and make it real. If so, we deepen the inner division and confirm our separation from each other.   Neither the inner schism nor its outward projection is real, yet we shall make them so in our minds if we hold onto our pain.

I am not telling you anything that you do not know. I am simply reminding you as I remind myself that all our spiritual concepts mean nothing if we do not integrate them into our lives. Our relationship is the laboratory for this work of integration. Every conflict we have offers us the opportunity to move beyond attack. Anything else we argue about is just superficial. Our real growth takes place in the depths of our being, where we come face to face with our primitive, raw, feelings of unworthiness and our hidden belief in our inequality.

~

A DREAM

In my dream, there are three birds. The birds are large and I am not entirely comfortable with them, but strangely I am more comfortable with these birds than I have been with birds in the past.

I look into the past, and I see that I have difficulty being in a room with birds flying around me. I can see myself cringing before their approach, dreading the touch of their wings, which I imagine as cold and clammy. The very thought of their touch repulses me. I feel pity for them, trapped in that enclosed space. But I too feel claustrophobic. The birds dominate the room with the frantic flapping of their wings. I try to find a place where I can be safe from them, but I cannot do so.

Birds are wild creatures, not pets, I feel. They belong in open spaces. I can admire them from a distance, as they dip, glide, and soar in the sky. They are wonderful symbols for freedom, and I like them as such. But I do not like them in a cage, especially if I have to share that space with them. That, to me, is a prison of the worst kind.

My past response to birds reflects fairly accurately my discomfort with my own emotions, having grown up in a household where emotional demands were constantly being made of me. My fear of their touch beautifully symbolizes my fear of my mother's love, which was always mixed with anger. Like the birds, she felt trapped. She had not honored her need for freedom and self expression. So her anger was very real. She was angry at me and angry at my father, who were apparently keeping her from actualizing herself.

Interestingly, the dream begins with much of this discomfort on my part being worked through. I am only slightly uncomfortable with the three birds that have been given to me. I seem to understand that I am ready to deal with the responsibility of having the birds as pets. I don't like this challenge, yet I don't feel the need to decline it. At any rate, it is clear that running away is not an option. I am in this room with the three birds and whoever has given them to me is helping me understand what I must do to take care of them.

165

The room is a large open space, two stories high, like a remodeled post-and-beam barn. I see that there is plenty of room for the birds to fly about. Still, they are large birds and I wonder how they will be able to fly, and what it will feel like when those large, cumbersome bodies become airborne.

I become aware that before they will fly, they need to develop trust in me and I need to develop trust in them. One of the birds flaps his wings and comes over to me, seeking to perch on my arm. His claws seem huge and I am a little afraid of them as they encircle me. Yet, I realize that he is not attacking me, but seeking to establish a relationship. He wants my love and acceptance. He too knows that it is time. I begin to relax with the task of learning to handle the birds. It seems okay. I see that they need me. My perception of their need is important because, no matter how uncomfortable I feel handling the birds, it helps me to understand that they mean me no harm.

This part of the dream accurately reflects my growing comfortability with my emotions and ability to begin taking responsibility for meeting my emotional needs. It also reflects the healing that has taken place in my relationship with both my mother and my father. Instead of blaming them for the past as I once did, I now take responsibility for the fear-based patterns I learned from them or in reaction to them. I see that they have freed themselves from many of these patterns and rejoice in that. My healing continues to be an internal process, appropriately reflected in my steadily improving relationship with each of them.

In the dream, I experience some anxiety about the

future. I become aware that I am a temporary guest in this room. I feel that I will not be here tomorrow. I will be moving somewhere else. What will I do with the birds, I wonder? This room is just perfect for them. I can take care of them here. But what happens if I have to move into a more confined space? That would be awful! Will I have to buy cages to transport them to the next space? The whole proposition of moving the birds seems overwhelming to me.

My silent teacher calms me down and helps me focus on the present. Today the room is here and it is perfect. Why be concerned about tomorrow? Who knows the duration of this event, or what the next one will be? I am here now and so are the birds. We need to get to know each other. We have work to do and the perfect opportunity to do it.

That, it seems, is all my dream wishes to convey to me. To be sure, I am afraid of what the future will bring. I am afraid to cross the bridge from this world to the next one. I am also afraid to cross the bridge in this life from illusion to reality.

I know that this is why I am here, but nevertheless I resist my lessons. Will I take these emotions with me when I go, or will they be released at last? I do not know. My guide assures me that it is not important.

"You are here," he says. "You have this opportunity to grow. It has been given to you because you are ready. You need not concern yourself with anything else but this. Choose to learn your lesson now, or postpone it. That is the choice, and you alone can make it."

A SECOND SKIN

All processes of transformation help us die to the old and give birth to the new. A caterpillar becomes a butterfly. A hermit crab abandons a tight shell for one that is roomier. Human beings let go of old fears so that they can learn to trust and express themselves in new ways.

That is the growth process. Every time we open our hearts, we cross an inner bridge to a fuller life. The situations that occur in our lives, especially those that appear to threaten our peace, offer us the invitation to learn, to grow, and to heal our wounds.

Growth is not easy, nor is it usually without pain. Yet if we seek to avoid pain, we arrest our growth. Ironically, the more we try to avoid pain, the more it deepens.

I have tried to show here that we cannot heal our wounds by pretending that they do not exist, nor can we heal them by dwelling on the pain they enclose. Our task is to recognize our pain as a cry for healing, and to liberate the pain from the mindset that holds it tightly in, inaccessible from conscious focus. Often, to release the pain, we must give ourselves permission to feel it.

The new skin that forms over the old wound is a sign that we have opened to our feelings and released them in the present. It is a sign that we have forgiven ourselves for the past and stopped carrying our guilt forward. Each of us has had profound experiences of healing our wounds, yet most of our healing does not come as a peak experience. It happens day by day, with every thought that we bring to truth, with every breath taken and released.

We have all witnessed the litany of projection. We have cried out "unfair" and "unjust." We have bitterly complained, to each other and to God. We have felt shame and cast blame. We have seen our own anger masquerade on our brother's face, and we have seen his anger walk unannounced into our dreams. We have held our hurt separately, and waged our battles to confirm our deepest fears.

Still, deep inside us, we know that we share a common wound. Deep inside, we know that we have nothing to prove, but only something to admit: "No, my brother, it is not you who attacks, but I. I attack myself, and it is of myself that I am afraid."

In my Book VIRTUES OF THE WAY, Spirit says:

"When the heart is calm,
the fish slips
from the hook.

When the mind is clear,
the bird breaks
from its cage
and dances in the heavens."

I did not know how prophetic those words would be when they were written in 1982. The hook is desire, and we desire only what we fear. Thus, we keep choosing it until, sooner or later, we overcome our fear and stop desiring what can never be ours.

Overcoming our fear of who we are is very deep work.

It requires great patience with ourselves and with our brothers and sisters. It also requires a growing mastery of the process of forgiveness.

To forgive you I must remember your sinlessness. Yet that will not help me unless I also remember my own, for it is not you I judge, but myself. Forgiving you is just a round-about way of forgiving myself for taking offense.

To forgive myself, I must go through all three steps of the process. I must recognize my error of self judgment, wish to change it, and be willing to let it go.

The birds in my dream will not be free until I have befriended them, allowed them to test their wings, and released them to the open sky. I cannot skip any of these steps if I would forgive myself for what I think I did, and love myself for who I really am.

~~

PATIENCE, COMPASSION, AND SELF-EMPOWERMENT

Our dignity as human beings depends on our patience and compassion for ourselves, as well as for our brothers. Practically speaking, this means understanding that we are all in different places on the same journey. One place is not further advanced or further behind than another. It is just where we are at the time. And because it is where we are, it is where we need to be.

If we want to grow, accepting where we are is essential. Learning happens from "the gut." Our gut always knows where we are, even if our ego doesn't. The ego's two favorite tricks are pushing us into situations for which we aren't ready and keeping us from taking risks we are ready to take.

Pretending to be ready for movement and new commitments when we are not brings us into emotionally threatening situations and relationships that demand more from us than we are able to give.

Attempts to take risks, express ourselves, or join with others before we have the inner strength and self confidence to do so usually backfire. We just disappoint others and weaken our own self-esteem. We need to work on accepting our current commitments more deeply and receiving greater nurturing and support from the people who already exist in our lives.

By contrast, pretending NOT to be ready for movement and new commitments when we ARE keeps us stuck in situations from which we need to extricate ourselves. The inability to let go of old securities and attachments overtaxes our relationships, invites co-dependence, and turns emotional supply into emotional scarcity. We simply cannot experience our independence and freedom to create our lives as long as we refuse to take risks and hold on fiercely to limiting roles and addictive relationships.

Holding back when we are ready to go ahead and racing ahead when we need to rest and to heal can be equally self-defeating. Each of these ego-dominated behaviors has its own psychological dynamic, yet both simply demonstrate a lack of love and compassion for ourselves.

Being loving and compassionate with ourselves sometimes means slowing down when we're going too fast. It sometimes means revving our engines to help us get out of old habits and emotional ruts. We need to accept the fact that we have not met our expectations or those of others. We need to accept the reality of shooting too high, or not shooting high enough, and learn from our mistakes. We need to relax and be at ease with our mistakes, for they are our teachers. We don't always know it, but they always lead us in the direction that is right for us at the time.

We all need to learn to trust our own life process, even though we don't always know where it is leading us. And we need to learn to trust our deepest aspirations and goals, even though we don't know how we will achieve them. Sometimes it may seem impossible to do this. And we will find ourselves straying from the beauty and integrity of our inner process, reaching outside of ourselves for some mental structure that will make everything fit into place, or looking to others for the approval we feel unable to give to ourselves.

This happens to all of us. We surrender our inner direction for an outside one. We sacrifice an inner possibility because it does not seem to be practical to others. We stop listening to the inner voice because its guidance seems too subtle or it does not speak loud enough. We would rather listen to a voice that commands rather than to one that gently prompts.

And so we lose touch with our inner authority. Instead, we project our power onto others. This is a game we cannot win, yet we all insist on playing it. Perhaps that is because it promises us wonderful results without asking for any work on our part. That is a very seductive proposition and we keep falling for it.

"This seminar offers enlightenment in just 30 days or a money back guarantee." It is hard for the children of

Madison Ave. to resist that kind of packaging. There is a guru for every temperament and a method of healing for every dominant belief. Which one is the right one? Which one delivers on its promises?

The truth is that they all deliver sometimes. But their success has more to do with the receptivity of the client than it does with the effectiveness of the treatment. The decision to grow or to heal is an internal one. Once that decision has been made, the client will spontaneously be led to whatever external agents, if any, can be helpful.

It is frequently said that, when the disciple is ready, the master appears. The master may be a blathering idiot or a God-inspired being. It doesn't matter. The truth is that he is right for this person in this situation. Thus, he answers the call.

Help is always available when we are willing to help ourselves. But no manner or degree of help will suffice if we are not ready to receive it.

~~

CHRIST VS. ANTI-CHRIST

When we do not accept ourselves, it is easy to project our power onto others. We like to think that other people have the answers to our problems, but that is just wishful thinking. Very few people have the answers to their own problems, much less the answers to ours.

Yet there are certainly plenty of people, who have not integrated their dark sides, who are willing to take our power from us if we offer it to them. We, in turn, do not see and believe in our own light. If we did, we would not look to others to "enlighten" us.

When someone accepts the role of "light-bearer" before he has wrestled with his shadow, he simply brings the shadow forward publicly. Promising light, he leads those who are foolish enough to follow him into a darkness deeper than the one they knew before they met him. Of course, they are as responsible for their situation as he is for his. He proclaimed himself "messiah" and they believed him. What they did not know is that only the Anti-Christ calls himself messiah, only the Anti-Christ promises to redeem us from our sins.

Contrary to popular opinion, Jesus did not die for our sins. He refused to recognize them. He saw the darkness, but he refused to make it credible. He saw our wound, our suffering, and our dis-ease, but he did not minister to them. He saw the creations of our belief, but he did not believe them. Instead, he showed us the truth about ourselves. Thus, he strengthened our light. He showed us our sinlessness.

Equality is the only kind of power we can receive from our sister. Equality proclaims: "What is in me is also in you." If there is any legitimate authority in all of Creation, it is the authority of equality. All other forms of authority are illusory. Whatever raises you above, or lowers you below your sister does not honor or empower you or her, but enslaves you both.

We reach an important place in our maturity when we finally realize that the solution to our conflicts is not found outside ourselves. Other people do not have the answers for us. All other people can legitimately do for us is support us in finding our own answers. That is real empowerment. That is the true gift of one brother to another.

TAKING A LOVE BATH

Loving and trusting ourselves requires that we learn to "tune in" to where we are and what we need at any point in our lives. It is a process of centering inside ourselves.

We all know how relaxing a bath can be. We immerse the body in warm water and it relaxes. It is cleansed and restored to its purity. In the same way, we need to learn to relax, cleanse and baptize our whole being, physically, mentally, and spiritually in the soothing waters of self-acceptance. In order to do this, we must allow ourselves to feel everything.

First, we start by feeling the physical body. We breathe deeply and calmly, focusing our awareness on each breath as it comes and goes, bringing warmth and softness to the places that feel tight, constricted, or ill at ease, and releasing any pain or tension we are feeling. Breathing in, we bring in warmth and softness. Breathing out, we release tension and constriction.

We thank our body for serving us. We express gratitude to our eyes for the gift of sight, to our lungs and vocal cords for the gift of breath and sound, to our arms and legs for the gift of extension, to our hands and feet for the gift of mobility and touch, to our ears for the gift of hearing, to our hearts and circulatory system for the gift of intuition and inner resonance, to our stomach and digestive system for the gift of nourishment and supply, to our intestines and eliminatory system for the gift of discrimination and detachment. We feel and bless all of the body and, as we do, we feel it lighten and relax. Our attention is now in the naval area, the body's center of gravity. The body feels alert, yet at rest, poised and at peace.

Then, we feel our mental/emotional body. We feel all of our thoughts and feelings, not just the ones we like but the ones we dislike and try to sweep away from conscious focus. We feel our conflicts without trying to resolve them and our expectations without trying to meet them; we feel our fears without running away from them and our desires without running toward them. We bless and soothe our mind with its complex array of thoughts and feelings. We accept all. We allow all the isolated and conflicting parts to sink down into the waters of wholeness. Slowly, gently, we allow our awareness to sink down into the heart center. There we feel unconditional acceptance for who we are. There we feel open, un-defended, trusting, and blessed.

Then, we extend this feeling slowly outward, imagining it as warm, soothing, golden light, radiating out from our heart center. We feel it expanding throughout our upper body, going down our arms. We feel its warm light radiate out from the palms of our hands and our fingertips. We feel the warmth and golden rays descending into our pelvis and down our legs. We feel it radiating out from our toes and the balls of our feet. We feel the light cross over the body's boundaries. We feel it radiating at the skin, at the hair, at the eyelids. We feel it in the breath we take in and release through our nose. Everywhere, we are surrounded by radiant, golden light.

Now, as we feel this warmth enfolding us, we allow it to extend outward gently to our brothers and sisters, enfolding them too in its embrace. We see our light joining with the light emanating from other beings. And, as we sense this joining, we feel the light and the warmth intensify.

We see that this light is infinite and unbounded. The circle is forever open and includes all beings within it. This is the circle of compassion that begins in our hearts and extends through every heart that beats in the universe. This infinite circle is the heart of God in which we all abide. No one is excluded here. All are welcome. All beings belong here with us, in oneness and unity.

And so our sense of unity deepens and expands until we feel connected with all creation. With each breath we take and release, we bless our brothers and sisters and are blessed by them. We feel this now. We feel the presence of the Holy Spirit here with us now. We see and know Her as our combined light, our combined love, for that is what She is. To Her we surrender any thought or feeling that troubles us, any problem, conflict, dis-ease, or sense of lack. Into Her circle of light and grace, we bring all feelings of separation, all needs for healing and release from pain. Into this radiant circle of light, we surrender all fear and any thought that we need do anything about our problems. Deeply we know that we need do nothing, for by the strength of our love for one another, are we healed and made whole. By our unconditional acceptance of ourselves and each other, which we now feel, is our abundance demonstrated.

Into this circle of acceptance do we bring all beings who feel lack of any kind that they may see and know that they are free of limits of any kind. Here healing is, for here is love's presence, and where love's presence is, there is all manner of health and well-being restored to those who mistakenly thought they had lost it.

Here there is nothing but warmth and light, acceptance and love. In this graceful circle we dwell for as long as we like, feeling our connection with all beings and with our Eternal Source. We dwell here in the heart of love, extending our love without limit and experiencing ourselves as an extension of love. We are all one body now, the body of Christ, the embodiment of love. We are all one purpose now, and one faith. Thus, we are at peace. Thus, do we feel that we have returned home.

Every day we should take such a love bath. It does not take more than fifteen or twenty minutes of our time. It recalls us to who we are and strengthens our connection to each other and to our Source. It establishes a regular practice of loving ourselves, accepting ourselves, and finding bliss in our own hearts. Every time we perform this ritual, we will deepen our joy and compassion and intensify our awareness of our inner guidance.

~

FEAR AND THE WINGS OF LOVE

I am afraid of the bird of prey. He is a carrion bird. He lives on blood and plunder. I think he exists only in my brother, but I am wrong. In truth, he exists in myself.

He is my fear personified. He is my self-judgment portrayed. See how he is poised to attack? I know that pose all too well. Yet when he reaches for you, it is I who feel pain. His beak is on my skin. I am the one he plunders and betrays.

All external conflict in my life comes from an adversarial relationship with myself. I do not like myself, so I attack myself. This bird of prey is just a symbol for me of that attack.

In my dream, I was ready to handle this bird, for by then I knew he was not someone separate from myself. And so I allowed him to approach, even though I was still afraid.

As he clumsily reached to encircle my wrist with his long talons, I became aware that I needed to relax. I needed to trust. If I did, he would come to rest gracefully on my arm. He would feel safe with me and I with him.

On the other hand, if I struggled, if I resisted the touch of his claw, if I forgot for a moment that that claw came in search of love, then my fear would awaken his. Then, he would become nervous, and his claw would re-open the wound.

Every situation in my life is like this one. In my fear of the claw, I forget the wing. Yet each has its function. One keeps me safe and brings me home. The others helps me grow and know my freedom.

The wings whose touch I fear are the same wings that lift me up when I have accepted the loved-starved child within. And in that moment of self-acceptance and forgiveness, the boy brings forth the gentle spirit in the man, and the carrion bird becomes the dove of peace.

In that moment of synergy, I stand face to face with myself, and say that I am worthy of love. And what I believe and say about myself is what I become. Thus, do the claws of judgment slip away and the wings of love enfold me and lift me from my fears.

"In our humanity we meet and discover that God is there with us. Divinity manifests through a human form. Perfection flowers in an imperfect world. Love lives in the lessons I learn and share."

IDEAS LEAVE NOT THEIR SOURCE

The work of integrating the dark side is not easy. There are no shortcuts or quick fixes on the path. Every fear we have must be faced. And we must feel the effect of every thought that we think.

This is not easy or superficial work. Self-hatred is not easily transformed into self-love. For with self-hatred come all the feelings of unworthiness that drag us down into darkness and despair. Yet if we can acknowledge this central feeling of unworthiness and turn it around, then we can heal our wounds and have the strength to change our minds about who we are.

This is our task and our happiness depends on our fulfilling it. Here and now, we take up the mantle of our growth. Ours is a heroic journey in search of Self. And in seeking who we are, we can be sure that we will meet our brother. And, in that meeting, will our gentle Guide appear, and help us cross the Bridge from the unreal to the real, from desire to acceptance, from fear to love.

Paul Ferrini's unique blend of radical Christianity and other wisdom traditions, goes beyond self-help and recovery into the heart of healing. He is the author of twenty-one books including his latest books *I am the Door, Reflections of the Christ Mind* and *The Way of Peace*. His Christ Mind Series includes the bestseller *Love Without Conditions, The Silence of the Heart, Miracle of Love* and *Return to the Garden*. Other recent books include *Creating a Spiritual Relationship, Grace Unfolding, Living in the Heart, Crossing the Water, The Ecstatic Moment* and *Waking Up Together*.

Paul Ferrini is the founder and editor of *Miracles Magazine* and a nationally known teacher and workshop leader. His conferences, retreats, and Affinity Group Process have helped thousands of people deepen their practice of forgiveness and open their hearts to the divine presence in themselves and others. For more information on Paul's workshops and retreats or The Affinity Group Process, contact Heartways Press, P.O. Box 99, Greenfield, MA 01302-0099 or call 413-774-9474.

Books and Tapes
available from Heartways Press

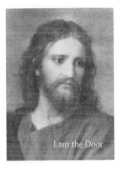

I am the Door
by Paul Ferrini
ISBN 1-879159-41-4
288 pages hardcover $21.95

Years ago, Paul Ferrini began hearing a persistent inner voice that said "I want you to acknowledge me." He also had a series of dreams in which Jesus appeared to teach him. Later, when Ferrini's relationship with his teacher was firmly established, the four books in the Reflections of the Christ Mind series were published. Here, in this lovely lyrical collection, we can hear the voice of Jesus speaking directly to us about practical topics of everyday life that are close to our hearts like work and livelihood, relationships, community, forgiveness, spiritual practices, and miracles.

When you put this book down, there will no doubt in your mind that the teachings of the master are alive today. Your life will never be the same.

Taking Back Our Schools
by Paul Ferrini
ISBN 1-879159-43-0 $10.95
This book is written for parents who are concerned about the education of their children. It presents a simple idea that could transform the school system in this country. This book does not pretend to have all the answers. It is the start of a conversation. It is chapter one in a larger book that has not yet been written. If you choose to work with these ideas, you may be one of the authors of the chapters to come.

The Way of Peace
A New System of Spiritual Guidance

Paul Ferrini

The Way of Peace
by Paul Ferrini
ISBN 1-879159-42-2
256 pages hardcover
$19.95

New

The Way of Peace is a simple method for connecting with the wisdom and truth that lie within our hearts. The two hundred and sixteen oracular messages in this book were culled from the bestselling *Reflections of the Christ Mind* series by Paul Ferrini.

Open this little book spontaneously to receive inspirational guidance, or ask a formal question and follow the simple divinatory procedure described in the introduction. You will be amazed at the depth and the accuracy of the response you receive.

Like the *I-Ching*, the *Book of Runes*, and other systems of guidance, *The Way of Peace* empowers you to connect with peace within and act in harmony with your true self and the unique circumstances of your life.

Special dice, blessed by the author, are available for using *The Way of Peace* as an oracle. To order these dice, send $3.00 plus shipping.

Our Surrender Invites Grace

Grace Unfolding:
The Art of Living A Surrendered Life
96 pages paperback $9.95
ISBN 1-879159-37-6

As we surrender to the truth of our being, we learn to relinquish the need to control our lives, figure things out, or predict the future.

We begin to let go of our judgments and interpretations and accept life the way it is. When we can be fully present with whatever life brings, we are guided to take the next step on our journey. That is the way that grace unfolds in our lives.

The Relationship Book You've Been Waiting For

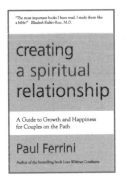

Creating a Spiritual Relationship: A Guide to Growth and Happiness for Couples on the Path

144 pages paperback $10.95
ISBN 1-879159-39-2

This simple but profound guide to growth and happiness for couples will help you and your partner:

- Make a realistic commitment to each other
- Develop a shared experience that nurtures your relationship
- Give each other the space to grow and express yourselves as individuals
- Communicate by listening without judgment and telling the truth in a non-blaming way
- Understand how you mirror each other
- Stop blaming your partner and take responsibility for your thoughts, feelings and actions
- Practice forgiveness together on an ongoing basis

These seven spiritual principles will help you weather the ups and downs of your relationship so that you and your partner can grow together and deepen the intimacy between you. The book also includes a special section on living alone and preparing to be in relationship and a section on separating with love when a relationship needs to change form or come to completion.

Return to the Garden
Reflections of The Christ Mind,
Part IV
$12.95, Paperback
ISBN 1-879159-35-X

"In the Garden, all our needs were provided for. We knew no struggle or hard-
ship. We were God's beloved. But happiness was not enough for us. We wanted the freedom to live our own lives. To
evolve, we had to learn to become love-givers, not just love-
receivers.

We all know what happened then. We were cast out of
the Garden and for the first time in our lives we felt shame,
jealousy, anger, lack. We experienced highs and lows, joy
and sorrow. Our lives became difficult. We had to work hard
to survive. We had to make mistakes and learn from them.

Initially, we tried to blame others for our mistakes. But
that did not make our lives any easier. It just deepened our
pain and misery. We had to learn to face our fears, instead
of projecting them onto each other.

Returning to the Garden, we are different than we were
when we left hellbent on expressing our creativity at any
cost. We return humble and sensitive to the needs of all. We
return not just as created, but as co-creator, not just as son
of man, but also as son of God."

Learn the Spiritual Practice
Associated with the Christ Mind Teachings

Living in the Heart The Affinity
Process and the Path of
Unconditional Love and Acceptance
Paperback $10.95
ISBN 1-879159-36-8

The long awaited, definitive book on the
Affinity Process is finally here. For years, the
Affinity Process has been refined by participants so that it
could be easily understood and experienced. Now, you can
learn how to hold a safe, loving, non-judgmental space for
yourself and others which will enable you to open your heart
and move through your fears. The *Affinity Process* will help
you learn to take responsibility for your fears and judgments
so that you won't project them onto others. It will help you
learn to listen deeply and without judgment to others. And
it will teach you how to tell your truth clearly without blaming others for your experience.

Part One contains an in-depth description of the principles on which the *Affinity Process* is based. Part Two contains
a detailed discussion of the *Affinity Group Guidelines*. And
Part Three contains a manual for people who wish to facili-
tate an *Affinity Group* in their community.

If you are a serious student of the *Christ Mind* teachings,
this book is essential for you. It will enable you to begin a
spiritual practice which will transform your life and the lives
of others. It will also offer you a way of extending the teachings of love and forgiveness throughout your community.

Now Finally our Bestselling Title on Audio Tape

Love Without Conditions,
Reflections of the Christ Mind, Part I

by Paul Ferrini
The Book on Tape Read by the Author
2 Cassettes, Approximately 3.25 hours
ISBN 1-879159-24-4 $19.95

Now on audio tape: the incredible book from Jesus calling us to awaken to our own Christhood. Listen to this gentle, profound book while driving in your car or before going to sleep at night. Elisabeth Kubler-Ross calls this "the most important book I have read. I study it like a Bible." Find out for yourself how this amazing book has helped thousands of people understand the radical teachings of Jesus and begin to integrate these teachings into their lives.

With its heartfelt combination of sensuality and spirituality, Paul Ferrini's poetry has been compared to the poetry of Rumi.

Crossing The Water:
Poems About Healing
and Forgiveness in
Our Relationships

The time for healing and reconciliation has come, Ferrini writes. Our relationships help us heal childhood wounds, walk through our deepest fears, and cross over the water of our emotional pain. Just as the rocks in the river are pounded and caressed to rounded stone, the rough edges of our personalities are worn smooth in the context of a committed relationship. If we can keep our hearts open, we can heal together, experience genuine equality, and discover what it means to give and receive love without conditions.

With its heartfelt combination of sensuality and spirituality, Paul Ferrini's poetry has been compared to the poetry of Rumi. These luminous poems demonstrate why Paul Ferrini is first a poet, a lover and a mystic. Come to this feast of the beloved with an open heart and open ears. 96 pp. paper ISBN 1-879159-25-2 $9.95.

Miracle of Love: Reflections of the Christ Mind, Part III

In this volume of the Christ Mind series, Jesus sets the record straight regarding a number of events in his life. He tells us: "I was born to a simple woman in a barn. She was no more a virgin than your mother was." Moreover, the virgin birth was not the only myth surrounding his life and teaching. So were the concepts of vicarious atonement and physical resurrection.

Relentlessly, the master tears down the rigid dogma and hierarchical teachings that obscure his simple message of love and forgiveness. He encourages us to take him down from the pedestal and the cross and see him as an equal brother who found the way out of suffering by opening his heart totally. We too can open our hearts and find peace and happiness. "The power of love will make miracles in your life as wonderful as any attributed to me," he tells us. "Your birth into this embodiment is no less holy than mine. The love that you extend to others is no less important than the love I extend to you." 192 pp. paper ISBN 1-879159-23-6 $12.95.

Waking Up Together: Illuminations on the Road to Nowhere

There comes a time for all of us when the outer destinations no longer satisfy and we finally understand that the love and happiness we seek cannot be found outside of us. It must be found in our own hearts, on the other side of our pain. "The Road to Nowhere is the path through your heart. It is not a journey of escape. It is a journey through your pain to end the pain of separation."

This book makes it clear that we can no longer rely on outer teachers or teachings to find our spiritual identity. Nor can we find who we are in relationships where boundaries are blurred and one person makes decisions for another. If we want to be authentic, we can't allow anyone else to be an authority for us, nor can we allow ourselves to be an authority for another person.

Authentic relationships happen between equal partners who take responsibility for their own consciousness and experience. When their buttons are pushed, they are willing to look at the obstacles they have erected to the experience of love and acceptance. As they understand and surrender the false ideas and emotional reactions that create separation, genuine intimacy becomes possible, and the sacred dimension of the relationship is born. 216 pp. paper ISBN 1-879159-17-1 $14.95

The Ecstatic Moment: A Practical Manual for Opening Your Heart and Staying in It.

A simple, power-packed guide that helps us take appropriate responsibility for our experience and establish healthy boundaries with others. Part II contains many helpful exercises and meditations that teach us to stay centered, clear and open in heart and mind. The Affinity Group Process and other group practices help us learn important listening and communication skills that can transform our troubled relationships. Once you have read this book, you will keep it in your briefcase or on your bedside table, referring to it often. You will not find a more practical, down to earth guide to contemporary spirituality. You will want to order copies for all your friends. 128 pp. paper   ISBN 1-879159-18-X $10.95

The Silence of the Heart: Reflections of the Christ Mind, Part II

A powerful sequel to *Love Without Conditions*. John Bradshaw says: "with deep insight and sparkling clarity, this book demonstrates that the roots of all abuse are to be found in our own self-betrayal. Paul Ferrini leads us skillfully and courageously beyond shame, blame, and attachment to our wounds into the depths of self-forgiveness...a must read for all people who are ready to take responsibility for their own healing." 218 pp. paper. ISBN 1-879159-16-3 $14.95

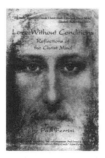

Love Without Conditions:
Reflections of the Christ Mind, Part I

An incredible book from Jesus calling us to awaken to our Christhood. Rarely has any book conveyed the teachings of the master in such a simple but profound manner. This book will help you to bring your understanding from the head to the heart so that you can model the teachings of love and forgiveness in your daily life. 192 pp. paper ISBN 1-879159-15-5 $12.00

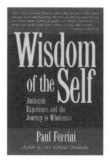

The Wisdom of the Self

This ground-breaking book explores our authentic experience and our journey to wholeness. "Your life is your spiritual path. Don't be quick to abandon it for promises of bigger and better experiences. You are getting exactly the experiences you need to grow. If your growth seems too slow or uneventful for you, it is because you have not fully embraced the situations and relationships at hand...To know the Self is to allow everything, to embrace the totality of who we are, all that we think and feel, all of our fear, all of our love." 229 pp. paper ISBN 1-879159-14-7 $12.00

The Twelve Steps of Forgiveness

A practical manual for healing ourselves and our relationships. This book gives us a step-by-step process for moving through our fears, projections, judgments, and guilt so that we can take responsibility for creating the life we want. With great gentleness, we learn to embrace our lessons and to find equality with others. A must read for all in recovery and others seeking spiritual wholeness. 128 pp. paper ISBN 1-879159-10-4 $10.00

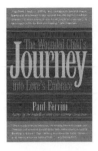

The Wounded Child's Journey: Into Love's Embrace

This book explores a healing process in which we confront our deep-seated guilt and fear, bringing love and forgiveness to the wounded child within. By surrendering our judgments of self and others, we overcome feelings of separation and dismantle co-dependent patterns that restrict our self expression and ability to give and receive love. 225pp. paper ISBN 1-879159-06-6 $12.00

The Bridge to Reality

A Heart-Centered Approach to *A Course in Miracles* and the Process of Inner Healing. Sharing his experiences of spiritual awakening, Paul emphasizes self-acceptance and forgiveness as cornerstones of spiritual practice. Presented with beautiful photos, this book conveys the essence of *The Course* as it is lived in daily life. 192 pp. paper ISBN 1-879159-03-1 $12.00

Virtues of The Way

A lyrical work of contemporary scripture reminiscent of the *Tao Te Ching*. Beautifully illustrated, this inspirational book will help you cultivate the spiritual values required to fulfill your creative purpose and live in harmony with others. 64 pp. paper ISBN 1-879159-02-3 $7.50

From Ego to Self

108 illustrated affirmations designed to offer you a new way of viewing conflict situations so that you can overcome negative thinking and bring more energy, faith and optimism into your life. 144 pp. paper ISBN 1-879159-01-5 $10.00

The Body of Truth

A crystal clear introduction to the universal teachings of love and forgiveness. This book traces all forms of suffering to negative attitudes and false beliefs, which we have the ability to transform. 64 pp. paper ISBN 1-879159-02-3 $7.50

Available Light

Inspirational, passionate poems dealing with the work of inner integration, love and relationships, death and re-birth, loss and abundance, life purpose and the reality of spiritual vision. 128 pp. paper ISBN 1-879159-05-8 $12.00

Poetry and Guided Meditation Tapes
by Paul Ferrini

The Poetry of the Soul

With its heartfelt combination of sensuali-ty and spirituality, Paul Ferrini's poetry has been compared to the poetry of Rumi. These luminous poems read by the author demonstrate why Paul Ferrini is first a poet, a lover and a mystic. Come to this feast of the beloved with an open heart and open ears. With Suzi Kesler on piano. $10.00 ISBN 1-879159-26-0

The Circle of Healing

The meditation and healing tape that many of you have been seeking. This gen-tle meditation opens the heart to love's presence and extends that love to all the beings in your experience. A powerful tape with inspirational piano accompaniment by Michael Gray. ISBN 1-879159-08-2 $10.00

Healing the Wounded Child

A potent healing tape that accesses old feelings of pain, fragmentation, self-judg-ment and separation and brings them into the light of conscious awareness and acceptance. Side two includes a haunting-ly beautiful "inner child" reading from The Bridge to Reality with piano accompani-ment by Michael Gray. ISBN 1-879159-11-2 $10.00

Forgiveness: Returning to the Original Blessing

A self healing tape that helps us accept and learn from the mistakes we have made in the past. By letting go of our judgments and ending our ego-based search for perfection, we can bring our darkness to the light, dissolving anger, guilt, and shame. Piano accompaniment by Michael Gray. ISBN 1-879159-12-0 $10.00

Paul Ferrini Talks and Workshop Tapes

Answering Our Own Call for Love

Paul tells the story of his own spiritual awakening: his Atheist upbringing, how he began to open to the presence of God, and his connection with Jesus and the Christ Mind teaching. In a very clear, heart-felt way, Paul presents to us the spiritual path of love, acceptance, and forgiveness. 1 Cassette $10.00 ISBN 1-879159-33-3

The Ecstatic Moment

Shows us how we can be with our pain compassionately and learn to nurture the light within ourselves, even when it appears that we are walking through darkness. Discusses subjects such as living in the present, acceptance, not fixing self or others, being with our discomfort and learning that we are lovable as we are. 1 Cassette $10.00 ISBN 1-879159-27-9

Honoring Self and Other

Helps us understand the importance of not betraying ourselves in our relationships with others. Focuses on understanding healthy boundaries, setting limits, and saying no to others in a loving way. Real life examples include a woman who is married to a man who is chronically critical of her, and a gay man who wants to tell his judgmental parents that he has AIDS. 1 Cassette $10.00 ISBN 1-879159-34-1

Seek First the Kingdom

Discusses the words of Jesus in the Sermon on the Mount: "Seek first the kingdom and all else will be added to you." Helps us understand how we create the inner temple by learning to hold our judgments of self and other more compassionately. The love of God flows through our love and acceptance of ourselves. As we establish our connection to the divine within ourselves, we don't need to look outside of ourselves for love and acceptance. Includes fabulous music by The Agape Choir and Band. 1 Cassette $10.00 ISBN 1-879159-30-9

Double Cassette Tape Sets

Ending the Betrayal of the Self

A roadmap for integrating the opposing voices in our psyche so that we can experience our own wholeness. Delineates what our responsibility is and isn't in our relationships with others, and helps us learn to set clear, firm, but loving boundaries. Our relationships can become areas of sharing and fulfillment, rather than mutual invitations to co-dependency and self betrayal. 2 Cassettes $16.95 ISBN 1-879159-28-7

Relationships: Changing Past Patterns

Begins with a Christ Mind talk describing the link between learning to love and accept ourselves and learning to love and accept others. Helps us understand how we are invested in the past and continue to replay our old relationship stories. Helps us get clear on what we want and understand how to be faithful to it. By being totally committed to ourselves, we give birth to the beloved within and also without. Includes an in-depth discussion about meditation, awareness, hearing our inner voice, and the Affinity Group Process. 2 Cassettes $16.95 ISBN 1-879159-32-5

Relationship As a Spiritual Path

Explores concrete ways in which we can develop a relationship with ourselves and learn to take responsibility for our own experience, instead of blaming others for our perceived unworthiness. Also discussed: accepting our differences, the new paradigm of relationship, the myth of the perfect partner, telling our truth, compassion vs. rescuing, the unavailable partner, abandonment issues, negotiating needs, when to say no, when to stay and work on a relationship and when to leave. 2 Cassettes $16.95 ISBN 1-879159-29-5

Opening to Christ Consciousness

Begins with a Christ Mind talk giving us a clear picture of how the divine spark dwells within each of us and how we can open up to God-consciousness on a regular basis. Deals with letting go and forgiveness in our relationships with our parents, our children and our partners. A joyful, funny, and scintillating tape you will want to listen to many times. 2 Cassettes $16.95 ISBN 1-879159-31-7

Risen Christ Posters & Notecards
11" x 17" Poster suitable for framing
ISBN 1-879159-19-8 $10.00

Set of 8 Notecards with Envelopes
ISBN 1-879159-20-1 $10.00

Ecstatic Moment Posters & Notecards

8.5" x 11" Poster suitable for framing
ISBN 1-879159-21-X $5.00

Set of 8 Notecards with Envelopes
ISBN 1-879159-22-8 $10.00

Heartways Press Order Form

Name _____

Address _____

City _____ State _____ Zip _____

Phone/Fax_____ Email _____

Books by Paul Ferrini

Taking Back Our Schools ($10.95)   _____
The Way of Peace Hardcover ($19.95)   _____
   Way of Peace Dice ($3.00)   _____
I am the Door Hardcover ($21.95)   _____
Reflections of the Christ Mind: The Present Day
   Teachings of Jesus Hardcover (Available May, 2000)   _____
Creating a Spiritual Relationship ($10.95)   _____
Grace Unfolding: The Art of Living A
   Surrendered Life ($9.95)   _____
Return to the Garden ($12.95)   _____
Living in the Heart ($10.95)   _____
Miracle of Love ($12.95)   _____
Crossing the Water ($9.95)   _____
Waking Up Together ($14.95)   _____
The Ecstatic Moment ($10.95)   _____
The Silence of the Heart ($14.95)   _____
Love Without Conditions ($12.00)   _____
The Wisdom of the Self ($12.00)   _____
The Twelve Steps of Forgiveness ($10.00)   _____
The Circle of Atonement ($12.00)   _____
The Bridge to Reality ($12.00)   _____
From Ego to Self ($10.00)   _____
Virtues of the Way ($7.50)   _____
The Body of Truth ($7.50)   _____
Available Light ($10.00)   _____

Audio Tapes by Paul Ferrini

The Circle of Healing ($10.00)   _____

Healing the Wounded Child ($10.00)   _____

Forgiveness: The Original Blessing ($10.00)   _____

The Poetry of the Soul ($10.00)   _____

Seek First the Kingdom ($10.00)   _____

Answering Our Own Call for Love ($10.00)   _____

The Ecstatic Moment ($10.00)   _____

Honoring Self and Other ($10.00)   _____

Love Without Conditions ($19.95) 2 tapes   _____

Ending the Betrayal of the Self ($16.95) 2 tapes   _____

Relationships: Changing Past Patterns ($16.95) 2 tapes   _____

Relationship As a Spiritual Path ($16.95) 2 tapes   _____

Opening to Christ Consciousness ($16.95) 2 tapes   _____

Posters and Notecards

Risen Christ Poster 11"x17" ($10.00)   _____

Ecstatic Moment Poster 8.5"x11" ($5.00)   _____

Risen Christ Notecards 8/pkg ($10.00)   _____

Ecstatic Moment Notecards 8/pkg ($10.00)   _____

Shipping

($2.50 for first item, $1.00 each additional item.   _____

Add additional $1.00 for first class postage   _____

and an extra $1.00 for hardcover books.)   _____

MA residents please add 5% sales tax.   _____

Please allow 1-2 weeks for delivery   TOTAL   _____

Send Order To: Heartways Press P. O. Box 99,
Greenfield, MA 01302-0099   413-774-9474
Toll free: 1-888-HARTWAY (Orders only)